THE SUCCESS OF
ELEVEN
JAPAN

JAPAN

Discovering the Secrets of the World's Best-Run Convenience Chain Stores

Akira Ishikawa
Aoyama Gakuin University, Japan

Tai Nejo

Published by

World Scientific Publishing Co. Pte. Ltd.
5 Toh Tuck Link, Singapore 596224
USA office: 27 Warren Street, Suite 401-402, Hackensack, NJ 07601
UK office: 57 Shelton Street, London WC2H 9HE

British Library Cataloguing-in-Publication Data
A catalogue record for this book is available from the British Library.

First published 2002
Reprinted 2007

THE SUCCESS OF 7-ELEVEN JAPAN (English translation)

Originally published in Japanese as
SEBEN-IREBUN DAKEGA NAZETSUYOI
in 1998 by The Sanno Institute of Management.

We would like to thank Seven-Eleven Japan Co., Ltd. for permission granted to use their corporate logo on the book cover.

ISBN 981-238-014-0
ISBN 981-238-030-2 (pbk)

Printed in Singapore by World Scientific Printers (S) Pte Ltd

Preface

"The era of dynamic change is now upon us." In this new age, consumer tastes have become ever more whimsical, demanding and diverse. Only the companies that can positively incorporate "change" as a major business and strategic ally will have the capabilities to survive the ruthlessness of this new high competition era. In practice, however, performing this feat is much easier said than done. How can "change" itself be made the key ingredient in the recipe of success? The core objective of this book is to find possible answers to this question through the exploration of the knowledge and insights generated by our detailed case-study analysis of 7-Eleven Japan.

As a standard bearer of revolution in logistics systems, 7-Eleven Japan has consistently been confronted with various business upheavals and uncertainties since its foundation in 1973. Indeed many upheavals have required 7-Eleven Japan to conduct some challenging reformations of its operations. Yet through these experiences, 7-Eleven Japan has clearly been able to establish a unique management concept. It has developed new management techniques and has created unique management systems that have enabled it to cope with the tumultuous changes of the time. Illustrations of these abilities are quite numerous.

It is said that the highly evaluated "*item-by-item management system*" as developed by 7-Eleven Japan was in fact the principal reason why gigantic retail groups such as Wal-Mart in the US and Metro in Europe made the decision to tie up with the Ito-Yokado group. It is also cited as the motivating factor as to why the usually reticent Chinese government openly granted the Ito-Yokado group a full retail license to operate in the Chinese market.

Apart from this particular management skill, 7-Eleven Japan has also been developing new epoch-making methods, to be discussed later, such as "*joint distribution*" and "*co-development*" well ahead of its competitors. Also the existence of the "*integrated information systems*" must not be overlooked when talking about 7-Eleven Japan's innovative and advanced management style. Integrated information systems play a key role not only in forming its corporate strategy but also in developing its functional strategies for logistic support, merchandising and store operations.

In this book, although we will spend many pages analyzing the integrated information systems of 7-Eleven Japan, it would be a little one-sided to claim that the source of the company's strong competitive power lies exclusively in the hardware used. It is very obviously the human elements who utilize the "integrated information system" and who actually run the organization helping it adapt to change. Therefore, we will focus on the importance of the management concepts of Hirofumi Suzuki, the charismatic owner of 7-Eleven Japan and pursue the reasons why 7-Eleven Japan has established itself as such a successful and particularly robust organization.

As there are so many valuable things to be learned from the management systems employed at 7-Eleven Japan, there already exists an absolute plethora of books praising and illustrating the company as the perfect enterprise. This is certainly not the purpose of this book. By using the business structural analysis model developed by Michael Porter, we are aiming for a very objective analysis and in addition to the excellence of the company, we will also look at some of the current problems and difficulties facing 7-Eleven Japan.

It is not only the inclinations of customers that have been rapidly changing in this industry. Several major external environmental factor transformations have occurred, such as industry deregulation and the emergence of a cashless society. These are central issues that could potentially dominate the future of 7-Eleven Japan. How can 7-Eleven Japan cope with these changes? In November 1997, 7-Eleven Japan adopted what is termed the "*fifth integrated information system*" for its stores as a measure to deal with the demands of this new era. We will clearly explain the features of this system that has allowed for such further progress and success.

So when you have finished reading this book, you will be aware of the reasons why in spite of the tough economic conditions, only 7-Eleven Japan has:

1. Achieved profits levels of over 111,000,000,000 yen — the first time such enormous profits have been achieved among retailers.
2. Exceeded its parent company in turnover and ordinary profits.
3. Managed to consistently surpass competitors for nearly 20 years since its foundation.

Moreover, you will get a clear idea on how the convenience store industry will continue to change and evolve in the 21st century. If this book could provide readers with a law for success in this "time of dynamic change", it would be a source of boundless joy for the author.

Finally, I would like to express my most sincere gratitude to Mr. Yoshio Nemoto, the publisher of Sanno University Press, who has been a constant source of valuable ideas and suggestions during the entire writing process of this book.

Contents

Chapter 1

"The Information Industry" Converting the "Change" into a "Chance"

Dealing with Changing Times, and 7-Eleven Japan's Continuing Self-reformations

A central business creed of 7-Eleven Japan is concerned with "dealing with the change of the times". 7-Eleven Japan, by making a friend of "change", has often managed to convert the change and uncertainty into a lucrative business chance. Perhaps it is more accurate to say that 7-Eleven Japan, by taking on the change of the times before others, has been able to better adapt due to a process of conducting rapid reformations of itself. "Change and reformation" are the keywords when analyzing 7-Eleven Japan. Since the establishment of operations in 1973, 7-Eleven Japan has performed several of these major reformations.

Firstly, we must look at the distribution system of the retail industry prior to the establishment of 7-Eleven Japan. The system was dominated by the major manufacturers and by their appointed wholesale stores. These appointed wholesale stores in turn handled goods made exclusively by those certain manufacturers. This did not match the requirements of 7-Eleven Japan who needed a flexible system with the ability to deliver products rapidly and whenever necessary. Therefore, 7-Eleven Japan created a wholesale store for every major area and established a distribution system called "*intensive delivery*". In this way, it became possible that products from multiple manufacturers were delivered quickly and efficiently to stores. This had the ancillary benefit of reducing the number of delivery vans required, which also contributed significantly to cost savings. This intensive delivery method has since developed into a system called "*joint delivery*" which became even more effective. This is the major first reformation/transformation performed by 7-Eleven Japan.

In the 1970's, 7-Eleven Japan was constantly expanding the overall number of stores. However, in the 1980's, a chronic situation of over-supply was apparent in the market. In addition, an increasingly diverse pattern of individualization among consumers had developed in the market and competition within the industry itself had greatly intensified. In order to cope with these changing external factors, 7-Eleven Japan pursued a core strategy of getting rid of non-selling products from the store shelves. To this particular end, 7-Eleven Japan developed the skill of "*item-by-item management*" and introduced POS (Point of Sale) technology, which was utilized as the primary tool for handling this management process. POS information was also directly used for new product development with the result that 7-Eleven Japan's ability to develop new products made very substantial progress. The introduction of "item-by-item management" by 7-Eleven Japan is worthy of being described as the second major reformation/transformation. It moved the competition of the convenience store industry from a "quantitative expansion" ideal to a more "quality improvement" type concept.

In 1990, 7-Eleven Japan established the "*fourth integrated information system*" which connected all chain stores using ISDN lines. As the transmission of large volumes of information became possible, other new services such as that of acting as the intermediary for payment acceptance were rapidly developed one after another. This meant the store was not only a place where products were sold but also a place that offered consumers several useful services. This change is the third major reformation achieved by 7-Eleven Japan. In 1997, the "*fifth integrated information system*" which connects all chain stores with a multimedia function started operation. As on-line image data transmission to member stores became possible,

Table 1-1. Response to changes and self-reformation

Changes in external surroundings (C) and measures by 7-Eleven Japan to changes (M) (before the 1960s)

- Dominance of distribution by manufacturers and appointed agents
- Rapid growth of supermarkets

....

(1970s)

C – Living environment at night changes
 (expansion of living time at night)
 – Management crisis of medium- and small-sized retail sectors
 – Enforcement of Large Scale Retail Store Law
M – Offering convenience (differentiation from other category of business)
 – Start of intensive delivery
 – Start of joint delivery
 – Speed-up of business (introduction of first integrated information system)
 – Development of multiple stores

....

(1980s)

C – Over-supply in the market
 – Individualization of consumption
 – Intensification of competition with rival firms
M – Differentiation in merchandise
 – Utilization of Point-of-Sale (POS) information (introduction of second and third integrated information systems)
 – Full-scale item-by-item management
 – ______________________

....

(1990s)

C – Long term recession
 – Intensification of inter-industry competition
 – Poor business performance of existing stores
 – Availability of ISDN line
M – Expansion of the service business
 – Sales of value-oriented merchandise
 – High-speed process of huge data (introduction of fourth integrated information system)

....

Table 1-1 (*Continued*)

(Toward the 21st century)
C – Progress of multimedia technology
  – Development of deregulation
  – Availability of electronic money
M – Store guidance by image data (introduction of fifth integrated information system)
  – Rapid expansion of business?
  – Movement into banking sector?

7-Eleven Japan could even pay closer attention to the education and information provision of its stores. One of the key features of this system is the ability it possesses to deal with the emergence of electronic money and business expansion. This fourth reformation has just begun and aims to assist 7-Eleven Japan's fortunes well into the 21st century. So in conclusion, it cannot be denied that 7-Eleven Japan indeed has a rich history of reformations.

Establishment of a Business Creed to Meet Social Change

In the early 1970's, the competition among small- to medium-sized retailers, department stores and supermarkets in the retail industry had greatly intensified. At this particular time, after experiencing the oil shock in 1973, the Japanese economy was at the turning point of moving from a period of high economic growth to a much slower rate of growth. It is worth pondering how 7-Eleven Japan accomplished such a successful entry to the retail industry under such unfavorable economic conditions.

In 1974, the "*Large Scale Retail Store Law*" regulating the set-up of large-scale retail stores and new rules on business hours was introduced. This law was primarily designed to protect existing small- to medium- sized retail stores. Essentially, it aimed to restrict the set-up of large-scale retail stores in prime shopping districts and other favorable locations such as train station squares. As a consequence, large-scale mass-market retail stores were forced to set up stores in less favorable locations in the outskirts of the city center and suburbs. However the small- to medium-sized retail stores, despite being under the protection of this new law began to lose their competitiveness due to inefficiency, lack of effort and the difficulty in finding successors to take over the business when they retired. As a result of this, many such shopping districts lost their customers and set off on the road to decline. Customers were instead attracted to the bigger stores in the suburbs. At this time, Ito-Yokado Co., Ltd. looked at the possibility of setting up small-sized stores that would not be in conflict with the "Large Scale Retail Store Law". However, they would be located in the prime shopping districts and other restricted key locations including train station squares. The exploitation of this legal loophole, so to speak, was also the reason why many other small-sized chain stores by the name of convenience stores were born.

Also at the same time big social changes were taking place in Japan. The expression "workaholic" became very common at this time, as many working men and women had become bound by very long working hours. There was a large element of personal sacrifice for the benefit and loyalty of the company to which they belonged. Some workers were even transferred away from their families to new company working locations. Other social changes included the increased amount of part-time work by housewives, and even young people tending to go to bed later than before was another factor. People's daily schedules became increasingly more busy and this left people with insufficient time to do shopping at their leisure. Convenience became the new buzzword. People tended to look for "*time convenience*" which would enable them to do their shopping at night. "*Convenience of being just around the corner*" which allowed them to do shopping near home or at least in the train station square. "*One-stop shopping*" gave shoppers the chance to purchase all the necessary things they wanted in one place. However, on the other side of the fence, the medium- and small-sized stores were not able to cope with these new demands from customers. It was the convenience stores who were able to bridge the gap. The concept of "*offering convenience*" simply could not be found in the conventional retail industry. Therefore, we must commend 7-Eleven Japan's foresight in spotting this change ahead of the pack and committing to the tie-up with Southland USA in order to launch the first group of full-scale convenience stores in Japan. So we can see that the business creed of 7-Eleven Japan of a "quick response to change" was already well practised even at the time of its establishment.

Converting "Problems" into "Opportunities"

At the time of rapid economic growth in the 1960's, supermarkets also enjoyed a period of rapid growth. However, this clearly posed a large threat to the management of medium- and small-sized retail stores of this time. As previously described the "Large Scale Retail Store Law" was supposed to protect the medium and small retailers by enforcing very strong regulation in the setting up of large scale retail stores in the shopping districts. A key management philosophy of Ito-Yokado Co., Ltd., a parent company of 7-Eleven Japan was "co-existence and co-prosperity". For Ito-Yokado Co., Ltd., not only "co-existence and co-prosperity" with suppliers but also "co-existence and co-prosperity" with the local community is very important.

Under the auspices of the "Large Scale Retail Store Law", Ito-Yokado Co., Ltd. judged that it was not possible to avoid opposition from the small- to medium-sized retail stores simply by setting up convenience stores. Therefore, it tried to minimize the number of stores under its direct management and deployed the strategy of the franchise system. The purpose of this strategy was to give local stores the opportunity to become convenience stores. This was considered a major contribution to the local community. Many small-sized stores lagged behind the times and have since been obliged to stop business completely or totally change their method of business. Therefore the franchise stores of 7-Eleven Japan offered good opportunities for the local stores to change to a method with a better chance of survival into the future. Generally speaking, franchise stores run by self-employed owners have much better results than stores that are run by salaried employees acting as the manager. Due to the franchise system, the burden of providing funds on the part of the headquarters could be minimized and the headquarters was able to obtain stores in the best locations. The higher ratio of franchise stores contributed to the high gains of 7-Eleven Japan. Therefore, 7-Eleven Japan converted problems of "co-existence" and "co-prosperity" to a "structure with high gains".

7-Eleven Japan Becomes an "Information Industry"

7-Eleven Japan could be viewed as an "information industry" in two ways. The first is due to the dependence of the headquarters on its satellite income sources and the second is the information system employed throughout the entire chain. Basically, 7-Eleven Japan consists of the headquarters and its member stores dotted all around the country. All member stores, except those stores under direct management of HQ, are franchise stores run by self-employed managers. The headquarters connect all member stores on-line and furnish them with sales results, inventory information, new product information, weather information and general information and know-how on store management. Member stores pay 40% to 45% of their total gross margin to headquarters as a royalty for their membership. Approximately 85% of headquarters total operating profit is composed of these royalties received from member stores. Therefore it seems quite appropriate to label 7-Eleven Japan as an "information industry" as most of the income is the reward for offering information and know-how.

Information and know-how is primarily transmitted from the headquarters to member stores via an integrated information system that connects all chain stores. The information systems of 7-Eleven Japan connect some 7,000 member stores and over 1,000 other business connections, making it the world's largest network in the retail industry. The headquarters make full use of POS information in order to control the strategy in the distribution of products and the strategy of individual stores. For member stores this integrated information system is an indispensable tool, especially for sales ordering procedures. Therefore 7-Eleven Japan is an enterprise with high dependence on information. It merits being classified as a "strategic information industry" judging from the features of its management style.

Using the Improvement of Information Technology to Conduct Self-reformations

Transaction volumes in the provision of the payment acceptance service of utility bills such as electricity and gas etc. amounted to nearly 300 million in 1996. Also the service range now extends to the payment acceptance of mail-order sales organized by Senjukai Co., Ltd. Although this service does not produce big profits itself, many customers are attracted to the store by this service. In addition, new sources of business using information systems such as payment by prepaid card etc. have also been extended. Since adopting the interactive POS system in 1995, it enables direct access to a host computer from a POS register. Before the store was a place for selling goods, but now it has become the place to offer many useful services by using the store information systems. It also contributes to a diversification of service. Therefore, it can be confidently stated that 7-Eleven Japan has honed the ability of converting new information technology into an immediate business opportunity.

It seems quite natural to observe the ever widening differences in the level of business performance of 7-Eleven Japan, who relentlessly continues its self-reformations, and the department stores and supermarkets, who are still having difficulties in breaking away from the conventional business structure.

A Subsidiary Company Whose Business Performance Has Exceeded Its Two Parent Companies

7-Eleven Japan actually has two parent companies. One is Ito-Yokado Co., Ltd. and the other is Southland Inc., USA, who offered their know-how and expertise at the time 7-Eleven Japan was established. When comparing the pre-tax profits and sales of 7-Eleven Japan with Ito-Yokado Co., Ltd. (see Table 1-2), the pre-tax profit of 7-Eleven Japan added up to 88.1 billion yen in February 1994 and in doing so, the profits actually exceeded those of its parents for the first time. Since then the business performance of 7-Eleven Japan has exceeded its parents for 4 consecutive terms. In February 1997, the pre-tax profit of 7-Eleven Japan broke the 100 billion barrier. Also the total sales of 7-Eleven Japan chain stores reached 1,609,007,000,000 yen, which exceeded the sales of Ito-Yokado Co., Ltd. In fact the sales figures of Ito-Yokado Co., Ltd. have been stagnant while 7-Eleven Japan has consistently shown more than satisfactory returns. It is therefore almost certain that the subsidiary company will remain ahead of the parent company for the foreseeable future.

In 1973, Ito-Yokado Co., Ltd. had a tie-up with Southland Inc. that was to introduce the American concept of 7-Eleven stores to Japan. In contrast to its US parent, 7-Eleven Japan has enjoyed continuous growth since its establishment, while Southland Inc. USA faced a major financial crisis in the late 1980's. The causes of Southland's business insolvency were due to its failures in the sectors of gasoline sales, oil business, urban development business as well as being a result of intensified competition in the convenience industry. Upon requests from Southland Inc., 7-Eleven Japan established operations in Hawaii and conducted a complete reconstruction of the Hawaii division. In fact, 7-Eleven Japan gained full control over Southland Inc. in 1991 and also started the reconstruction of Southland branches in Canada and mainland USA. Thanks to 7-Eleven Japan's management efforts of liquidating unprofitable stores and in introducing systems like the practice of

Table 1-2. Comparison of business performance of 7-Eleven Japan with Ito-Yokado Co., Ltd

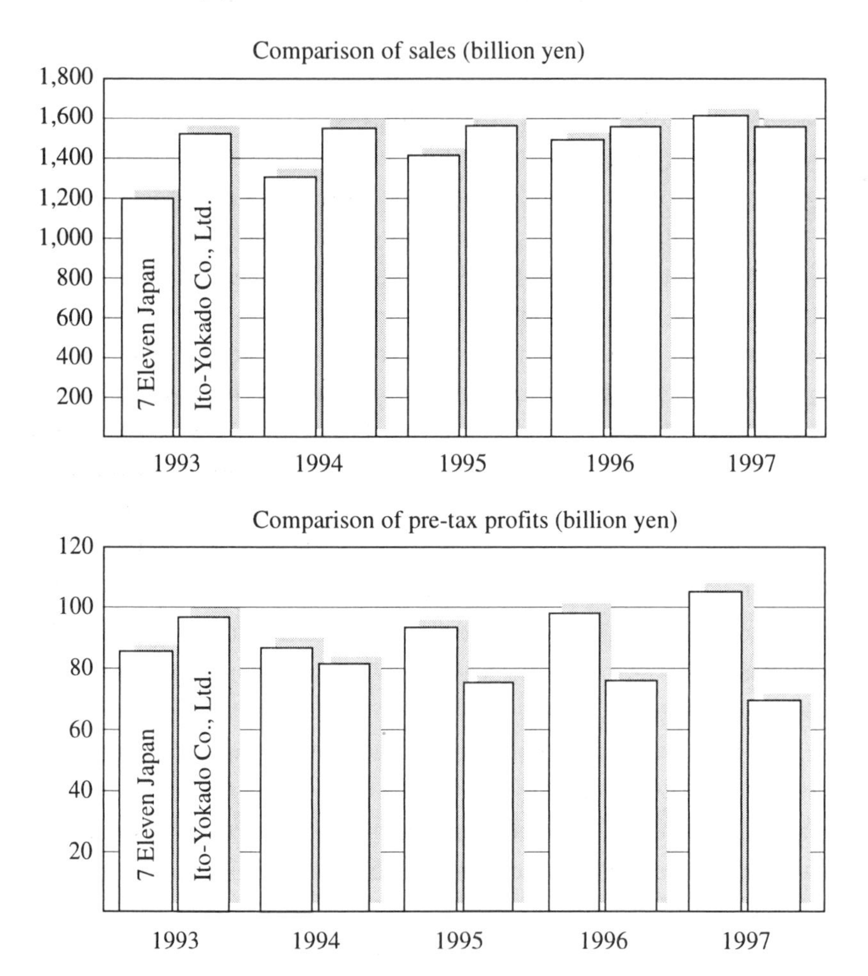

item-by-item management, it has succeeded in returning Southland's pre-tax profit to the black in 1994. Thereafter 7-Eleven Japan's reconstruction schemes are satisfactorily proceeding. This case represents not only "children" who have outgrown "parents" but also "children" who have saved the life of "parents". Therefore this attracts considerable attention as an excellent example of how the management know-how of 7-Eleven Japan could be used in the wider business world.

Definition of a Convenience Store

There is no one fixed definition of a convenience store. *Nikkei Ryuutsuu Shinbun* categorizes chains satisfying the following three conditions as a convenience store.

1. The sales composition ratio of perishable foods should be less than 30% of total sales.
2. Business hours per day should be more than 16 hours.
3. The majority of the department area should be less than 200 square meters.

Another definition comes from the MCR (Manufacturer Convenience Researcher) who specializes in researching convenience chains defines stores satisfying the following standards as proper convenience stores.

1. Retail stores with department area of more than 50 square meters but smaller than 230 square meters.
2. Shares of counter sales for general foods (including liquor and confectioneries) should be more than 50% of total sales.
3. Shares of counter sales of liquor, perishable foods, confectioneries, FF (fast food), lunch box, daily dishes and products other than foods should be less than 60% of total sales.
4. Business operations should be more than 14 hours a day and 340 days a year.
5. Stores should handle more than 1,500 items of convenience products and services.
6. The layout of the store should be the convenience style provided with unique energy savings, friendly atmosphere and measures for crime prevention.

7. There is no necessity for an individual to be a member of a chain store group or to be tied up with another business to fit in with this definition of a convenience store.
8. Combined type convenience connected with a different category of business would be collectively regarded as a convenience store, provided it corresponds to the following conditions. However, no stores that has more than 50 square meters for convenience section will be included in the definition.

A. Department area of different categories of business (including eat-in corner) should be less than 50% of the entire department area.
B. Incoming and outgoing activities between the department areas must be freely allowed in the store.
C. Regardless of decentralization of the cash register, the final accounting business should be unified.

Chapter 2

The Birth of "Item-by-Item" Management and the Integrated Information System

The "Item-by-Item Management" System of 7-Eleven Japan

When Yaohan Japan went into bankruptcy in 1997, the principal cause of business failure was said to be the deadlock of its business operations in China. The Yaohan Chinese operation was critical to the health of the entire company. Previously all had seemed well, as Yaohan Japan had been satisfactorily expanding its business in the China market — a good example being the opening of its department store "Next Stage" in Shanghai, the largest city in the East. However, the major blow came when instead of Yaohan Japan, the Chinese government granted a supermarket operation license for the Chinese market to the Ito-Yokado Group. This was the first time that the Chinese government had granted such a license to a foreign affiliated retail industry. It was a huge shock and a devastating blow to Yaohan Japan who had been very confident that it would acquire the license. What were the reasons behind this decision? The Chinese government had dispatched staff managers of the China National Export and Import Corp., to Japan to study the retail industry in Japan. The importance of the know-how of "item-by-item management", as practised by the Ito-Yokado Group, was discovered by these Chinese researchers. The power of this management technique was the simple reason why the Chinese government selected the Ito-Yokado Group to grant the lucrative license.

This "item-by-item" management tool is not possible without the support of the Point-of-Sale (POS) system. 7-Eleven Japan, using this excellent information system has in place a comprehensive item-by-item management system for nearly 3000 items on average per store. This system led to a substantial improvement in the accuracy of order placement. The skill to grasp the needs of customers for all kinds of merchandise was really a revolutionary practice management that had never been accomplished before. The fact that the "item-by-item" management practice and its information system was highly appraised by the Chinese government symbolizes the competitiveness of 7-Eleven Japan.

Synergistic Effects Generated by the Information System

7-Eleven Japan defines itself as "the company that offers convenience" with the following features of convenience being at the fore:

Time	Stores open 365 days with long business hours.
Distance	Availability of multiple stores, "always just around the corner".
One-stop shopping	Customers can buy all essential goods in just one place.
Quick shopping	The layout of the store is ideal for customers to locate their required products easily.
Reasonable price	Goods at reasonable prices (no practice of bargain sales).

In order to construct an effective offer of these "conveniences factors", 7-Eleven Japan developed an individual strategy for each good, each distribution mode and each individual store. However such systematic efficiency can only be attained with a harmonized operation for each strategy. 7-Eleven Japan considered information systems as the requisite tool for connecting each strategy in an organic way. Synergy effects generated from each strategy enhance the efficiency of its systematic operation. One of the secrets of 7-Eleven Japan's high gains is hidden within this structure.

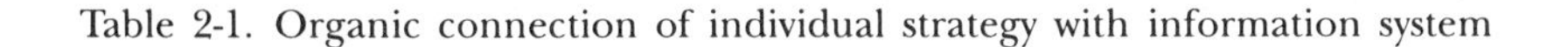

Table 2-1. Organic connection of individual strategy with information system

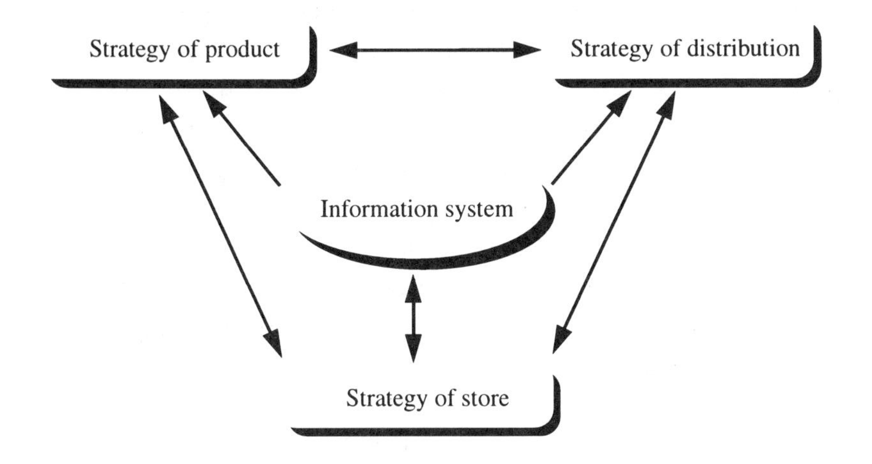

7-Eleven Japan has always been investing positively in the information system as the "center" of its strategy. Since introducing the first integrated information system connecting all the chains in 1978, it has been continuing to upgrade the system every few years and has now created the newest "fifth" integrated information system. 7-Eleven Japan invested 25 billion yen in the "fourth" integrated information system and 60 billion yen in the "fifth" information system. It could be said that the prosperity of the company allowed this investment to be fully self-financed. The robustness of 7-Eleven Japan's financial standing is one of the primary reasons why other competitors cannot catch up with it.

Rationalization Efforts Made Before the Introduction of the Integrated Information System

Pre-1978, the period prior to the introduction of the integrated information system is an interesting time to inspect. The total number of 7-Eleven Japan stores in 1975 was less than 100, but 7-Eleven Japan had more than 70 different vendors supplying it with products. Member stores placed orders by telephone with each vendor of the products they wanted, so it was a very time-consuming process. It was also a busy process dealing with countless order slips, shipment instructions, delivery statements and bills. Mistakes were often made due to simple misunderstandings from telephone conversations.

Therefore, 7-Eleven Japan started a "slip order" system in 1978 in order to simplify the business process concerning the placement and acceptance of orders. The new system of ordering took the following format:

1. The slip order consisted of pages for each product and the member store filled out the quantity desired of that product when ordering.
2. Pages already filled with quantities were torn out and compiled to be used as a daily order book for the member store.
3. The OFC (Operation Field Counsellor) visited member stores each day and collected their order books and then submitted them to the district management offices.
4. After punching the input of the member store number at the district management office, a computer at the headquarters printed out the purchase slip which was categorized by each vendor.

Table 2-2. Changes in the number of stores

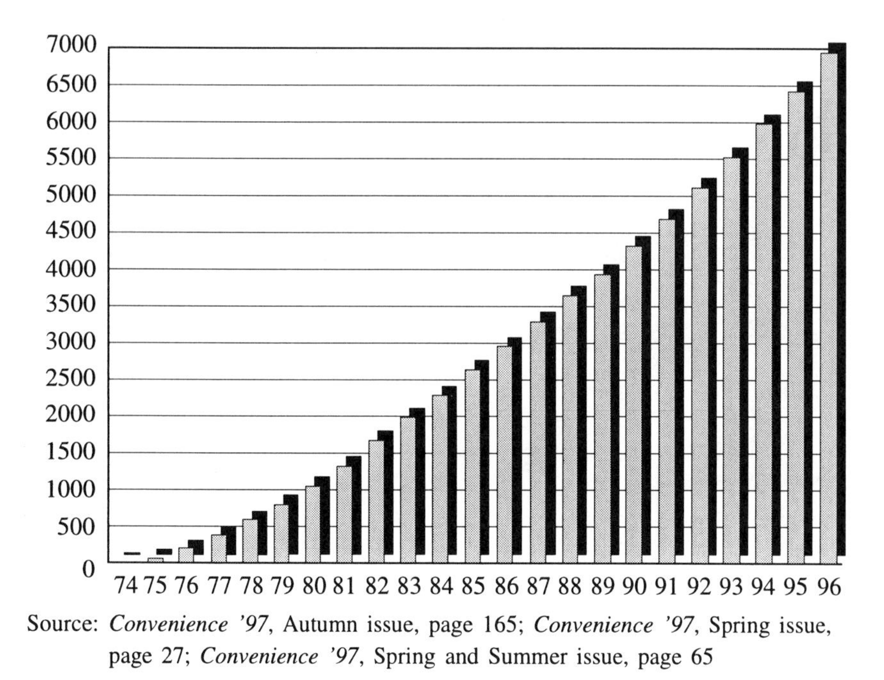

Source: *Convenience '97*, Autumn issue, page 165; *Convenience '97*, Spring issue, page 27; *Convenience '97*, Spring and Summer issue, page 65

5. Each vendor visited the headquarters and collected the purchase slip.

Using this new method of handling, mistakes made during the telephone ordering were eliminated and the time-consuming nature of order processing was greatly reduced. Compared to today's ordering process, the rationalization of order handling business by slip-order seems quite "primitive". However, this was the starting point from which the excellent information system was developed.

Introduction of "Terminal Seven"

The utilization of a "slip-order system" greatly improved the clerical procedures of ordering and order-acceptance. However, this system

Table 2-3. On-line order placements by terminal seven (1978)

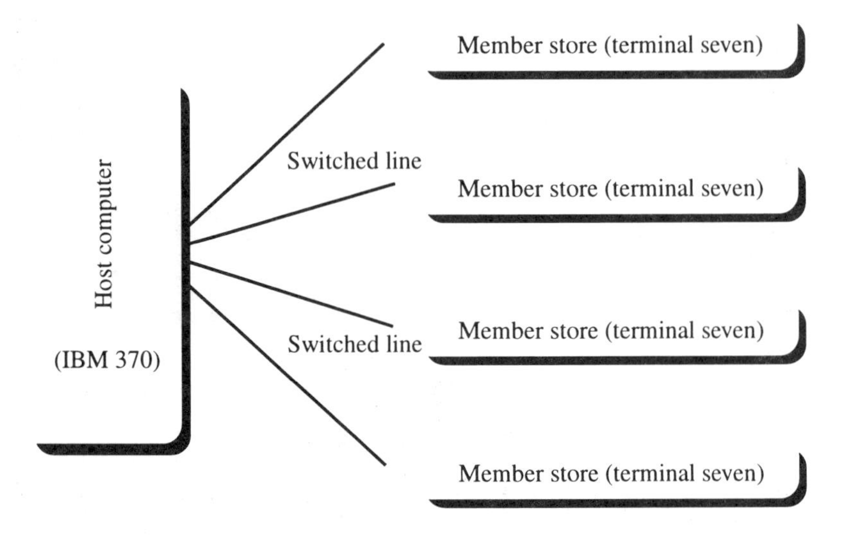

required daily visits by an OFC to the chain stores in order to collect order books and submit them to the regional office governing the area. In this regard, there was much scope left for further rationalization of the ordering system. 7-Eleven Japan had yet to connect ordering information on-line. As Table 2-2 shows, the number of 7-Eleven Japan chain stores reached almost 400 in total by 1977. In order to make good use of the concept of "offering convenience just around the corner", it was necessary to expand the numbers of chain stores but this "slip order system" dependence on human elements had obvious limitations.

In 1978, 7-Eleven Japan introduced a terminal machine called "Terminal Seven" which was used for creating a new ordering procedure. It connected the headquarters with the chain stores on-line. As a result of this, the transmission of order information, between the headquarters and chain stores became possible without the use of human intermediaries. The order procedure of "Terminal Seven" was as follows:

- After scanning the bar codes of order items, the order quantity and the name of vendor, etc. by using a pen-reader (scanner) that was linked to a Terminal Seven, all subsequent data is input into the main body of the terminal seven.
- Data is transmitted to a host computer from a Terminal Seven by a switched line.
- The headquarters compiles orders from chain stores per vendor and prepares the order slips.
- The headquarters mails the purchase slips or the vendor comes to the headquarters to pick them up.

Thanks to on-line data transmission between the chain stores and headquarters, the clerical work volume at the store was drastically reduced and the daily visit by the OFC to chain stores

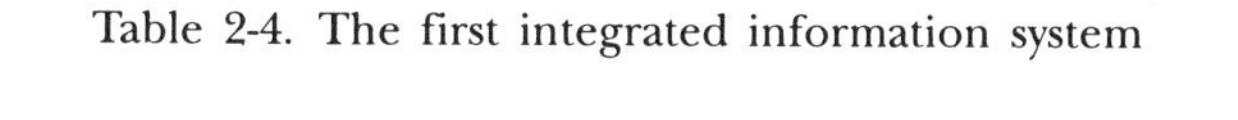
Table 2-4. The first integrated information system

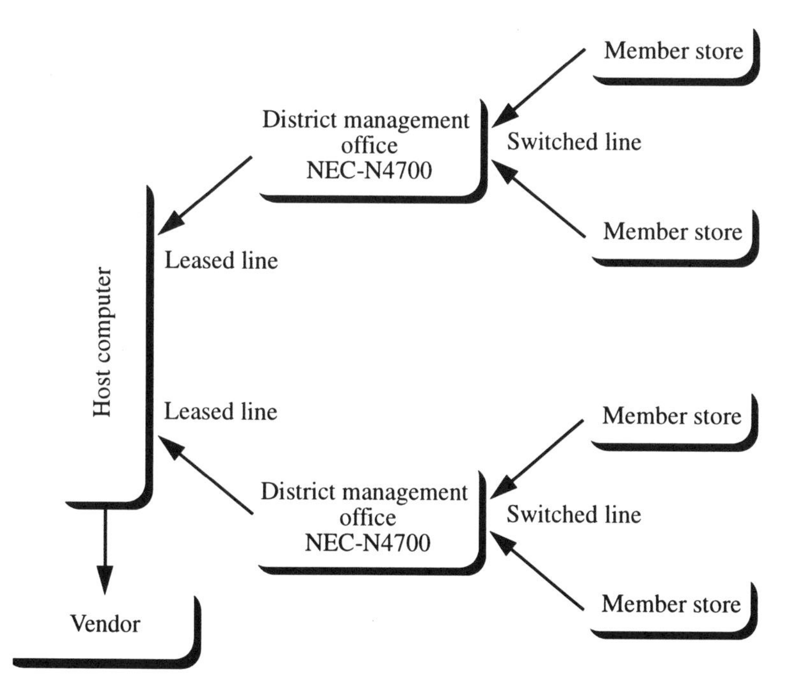

became unnecessary. However, the headquarters and the vendor were still not connected on-line and procedures of ordering and the acceptance of orders were carried out by mail or by the visit of a person in charge.

First Integrated Information System Enables the Expansion of Multiple Stores

The on-line transmission of order information to vendors had not been possible because networks linking independent business groups were strictly prohibited by law. However the construction of exclusive networks was finally approved due to the revision of Law in 1979. 7-Eleven Japan requested the Nomura Computer Systems group to develop a network for her exclusive use. This 7-Eleven Japan information system had specific features of a network of the distributed processing type. A computer of the distributed processing type: NEC-N4700 was stationed at five (5) regional offices. A switched line transmits ordering information from the chain stores to a regional office. From regional offices to headquarters, information was transmitted by a common carrier leased line. Due to this distributed processing, risks in times of trouble were avoided. In addition, the lead time from ordering to delivery was shortened drastically because of the establishment of the network with vendors.

In the 1980's, a new system of an order ledger, a new model of terminal seven, and on-line accounting systems were created. Thus the first integrated information system was further improved. With the employment of the first integrated information systems connecting all chain stores, 7-Eleven Japan was to expand and open many new stores. Therefore, 7-Eleven Japan established itself in the dominant position of the convenience industry even at that developing stage.

Transforming "Disadvantageous Changes" Into Advantages

In the 1980's, all retailers including the convenience industry encountered a situation of "over-supply" on the market. Consumers became more careful in their shopping and tended to buy only the bare necessities. Even 7-Eleven Japan experienced a lower rate of increase in sales and profits from 1981 during this period. Thus 7-Eleven Japan experienced this harsh negative market change. Trends in inventory turned flat and the stagnant atmosphere among member stores worsened with the opinion "that it is not possible to decrease inventory more than the present level".

7-Eleven Japan considered the reasons for this slowdown in improvement was caused by improper order practices by member stores and the lack of the same kind of passion and enthusiasm as at the time of establishment. When member stores ordered without correct knowledge of customer's needs, the disposal loss of unsold products had increased and the loss of sales opportunities also increased because of a lack of certain stocks. Furthermore, some stores did not grasp the lost volume of sales opportunities. In order to expand the sales figures, focusing on "heavy-selling items", and preventing stock-out situations was rather critical. This meant it was important to get rid of "poor-selling items". However, it must be noted that sales data to prevent the problems mentioned above were poor and mostly unavailable at that time.

It became necessary to prepare sales data per customer group, for each shopping time zone, for every single item and for every store as each store have very different conditions of location and customer base respectively. Without such arrangements of sales data, the analytical work to survey the causes of disposal loss and the loss of sales opportunities were not possible. The collection of huge sales data only by manual means was just not possible. This is the main reason why 7-Eleven Japan introduced the "second" information system linked with the POS system in 1982. As stores used the POS information for "item-by-item management", bad inventory was reduced and thus the arrangement of only the heavy-selling items in the store became possible. As a result, as Table 2-5 shows, the sales figures of member stores increased again and the volume of inventory decreased.

Table 2-5. Changes in the management index of 7-Eleven Japan

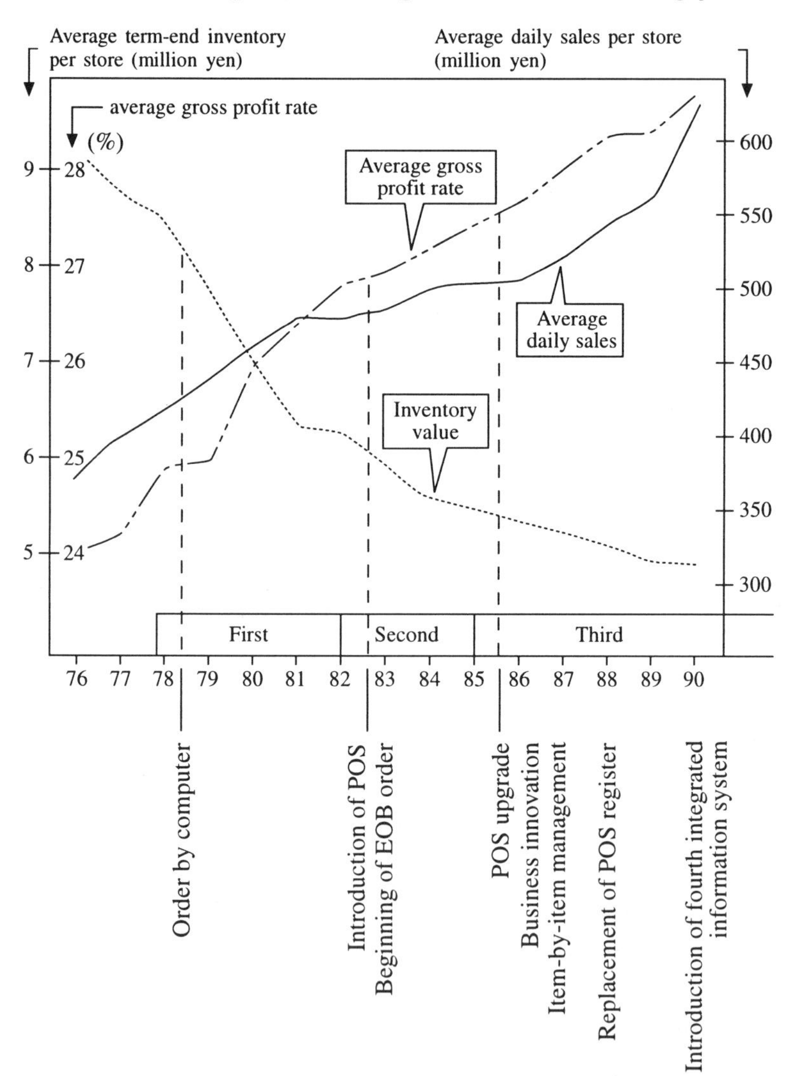

Source: *7-Eleven Japan's Endless Innovation*, page 196

The purpose of the first integrated information systems connecting chain stores was to achieve a rationalization of work and improve working efficiency. However, the second integrated information systems was used as a tool to carry out "item-by-item management", which was very significant. The POS system is now an indispensable system in the retail industry and "item-by-item management" is a management skill that has worldwide potential.

Each convenience industry has introduced a POS information system in the following years:

7-Eleven Japan	1982
Mini-stop	1987
Lawson	1988
Family Mart	1989

7-Eleven Japan paid careful attention to this system at the earliest stage. Its foresight and progressive spirit brought about a superior position in the competition among the convenience industry. Thus 7-Eleven Japan made good use of the times of over-supply, "the disadvantageous change" was used positively to develop new information systems and management skills. Its management philosophy of responding to changes and continuing self-reformations are well represented by the second integrated information systems.

The Second Integrated Information System Available for Marketing Purposes

The second integrated information system was an open system connecting member stores, regional offices, headquarters and vendors whose central operating function was based on the POS system. Data was transmitted on the solid lines shown in Table 2-6. Bar code indications were indispensable for POS. The vendor's POS labeling systems had first operated in 1982. Machines and

Table 2-6. The second integrated information system

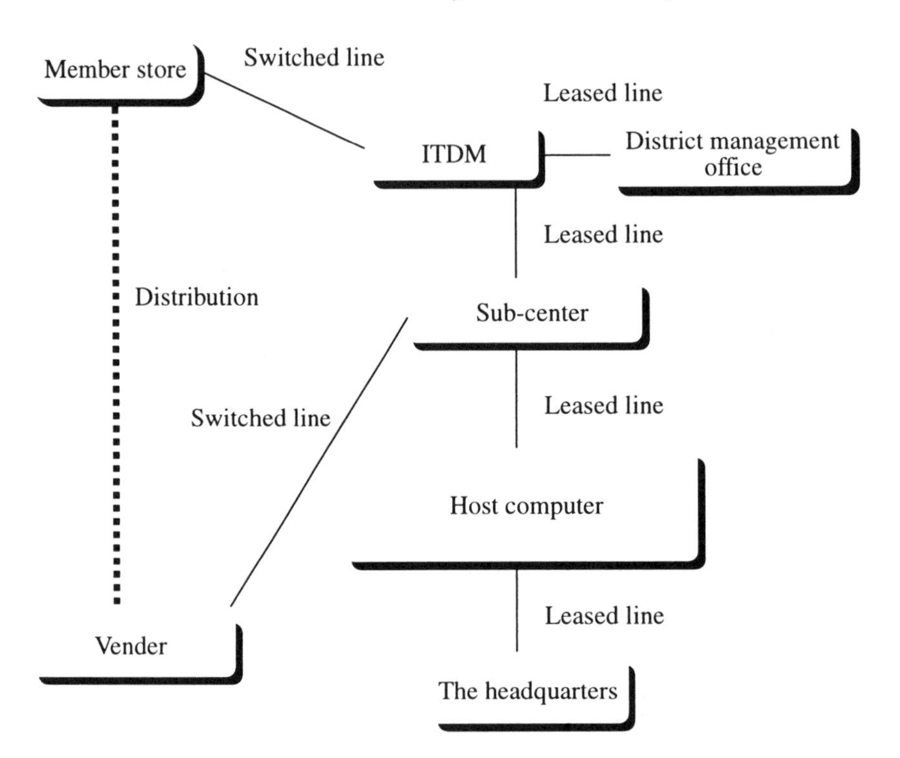

Source: *7-Eleven's Revolution on Information System (7-Eleven no jouhou kakumei)*, page 95

equipment were manufactured with the concept of "ease of operation", "miniaturization", "cost savings", and "extensiveness". In particular, the portable electronic order book and EOB (electronic order booking terminal) were innovative and epoch-making products.

(a) The SC "Store Controller"

The terminal controller stationed at the store is connected to the POS register, the personal computer, and EOB etc. In addition, the functions for controlling store temperature and lighting, printing, crime prevention surveillance systems were also built-in. Along with these functions the store outside communications was also carried out via this store controller. It used a floppy disk and both M-type floppy and T-type floppy disks could be used in this terminal controller. The M floppy disk had part of the memory of the master file with the headquarters input and the controller starting program. The OFC brings this floppy disk to member stores once a week and replaces the old one.

Data input by a touch scanner equipped with a POS register is accumulated in the T floppy. The OFC replaces the T floppy which is already full of data twice a week. The store controller automatically collects and processes data on campaign merchandise. This information is transmitted when member stores send their order data. Member stores can print out daily sales volume per each single item, the number of customers for every group, and total sales amounts from the printer of the store controller.

(b) The POS register

Usually two sets of POS register with a hair-dryer type scanner are stationed in the store.

(c) The EOB (Electronic Order Booking) terminal

Two sets of electronic order booking terminal are stationed in each store.

Before this terminal was introduced, the person in charge carried a thick bar-code book and order quantity cards to input order information by pen scanner with nearly 3000 kinds of selling items. Obviously, this was very time-consuming and very hard work. Therefore a handy (the carrier was only 12 cm in width) and lightweight (280 grams) EOB was developed so as to minimize this order input work. This was very compact and easy to carry. The handy type is not only convenient to carry but also has the advantage that data input is indicated on the liquid crystal display screen. The terminal displays the following data:

Data on "goods to be ordered"

Delivery requirements
Sales period
Minimum inventory quantity
Gross margin rate
Delivery day
Name of delivery van
Sales price recommended by headquarters
Order unit
Minimum order quantity
Sales ranking
Markings per delivery day (weekdays, Sundays, public holidays, no delivery on the following day)
Order quantity

Data on "orders in the past week"

Order record per day in the past week
Delivery quantity
Disposal record

The ordering data is transmitted on-line from a store controller via ITDM, sub-center to the vendor. The POS information of the store is to be added up at the headquarters each week and compiled as data for every single article. The OFC will bring this compiled data sheet to member stores. The analytical information consists of the following data:

1. Inventory list per member store and day
2. Reports on merchandise
3. Merchandise trend analysis (the cost of every single article, rebate and selling price. Sales composition ratio, gross profit ratio, gross profit composition ratio)

Furthermore, the OFC brought a balance sheet and profit and loss statement for all member stores prepared by the computer at the headquarters. From 1983 when digital picking started at the joint delivery center, workloads have been drastically reduced.

The second integrated information systems connecting chain stores is characterized by the desire to attain working efficiency and availability in the use of this information in marketing. "Item-by-item management" developed by 7-Eleven Japan is the source of strong competitiveness. The second integrated information system was of key significance because it made the item-by-item management system technically possible.

Responding to the "Individualization of Consumption" with Graphic Information Analysis

In the mid-1980s, new industry changes in the form of the "individualization of consumption" became prevalent. In affluent times, consumer's preference and needs tend to become more diversified. Since each member store of 7-Eleven Japan has different geographical conditions and customer bases, it is unable to meet all the diversified needs of customers by simply arranging the same selection of merchandise for all chain stores. In order to satisfy the individualized and diversified needs of consumers, each store must pay full attention to order placement and the selection of merchandise. That is why 7-Eleven Japan had to practise item-by-item management in a full-scale way. Under the second integrated information systems, "item-by-item management" produced good results in its own ways but also created problems. As the POS information of member stores was processed and added up after the headquarters collected them in a floppy disk, data were available only one week after processing. Furthermore, POS data was quite difficult to interpret as it was a complex lot of figures on a sheet. Member stores did not fully utilize them contrary to headquarters' expectations. Therefore, it was a task of 7-Eleven Japan to help member stores utilize the POS data as often as possible. When the third integrated information system was introduced in 1985, 7-Eleven Japan ordered a computer with the ability to indicate graphic information for easier interpretation. Due to this visualization of information, an effective way of using POS data was created and the ordering accuracy of member stores has improved. As Table 2-2 shows, the average daily sales of member stores have rapidly improved, which is a good effect generated directly by the third integrated information system.

In order to respond to the change of the "individualization of consumption", 7-Eleven Japan replaced the second integrated information system with a new system in less than 3 years. So the third integrated information system symbolized how speedy 7-Eleven Japan conducted its self reforms.

Differentiation of Product Quality to Cope with "Intensification of Intra-Industry Competition"

In the mid 1980s, other major "changes" together with the "individualization of consumers" had been taking place. As Table 2-7 shows, the total number of stores in the convenience industry reached over 30,000 stores in 1986. Until then, 7-Eleven Japan had made an excellent impact in the retail industry due to its policy of differentiation from other categories of business such the supermarkets. However, the competition with rival companies was intensified due to the new entry of Lawson, Family Mart as well as many other small- and large-sized convenience stores.

7-Eleven Japan developed a new strategy to deal with this change which aimed to attract customers by achieving a differentiation in products. This meant a conversion of strategy from "quantitative expansion" to "quality improvement" so as to offer attractive merchandise. In order to materialize "quality improvement", 7-Eleven Japan had to grasp customer's needs in details and in quicker and correct ways. The third integrated information system was highly compatible to this goal. Thus, 7-Eleven Japan made positive use of the information obtainable from POS for the development of new products. Methods of "co-development" contributed greatly to the birth of many successful products, such

Table 2-7. Changes of number of stores in the convenience industry

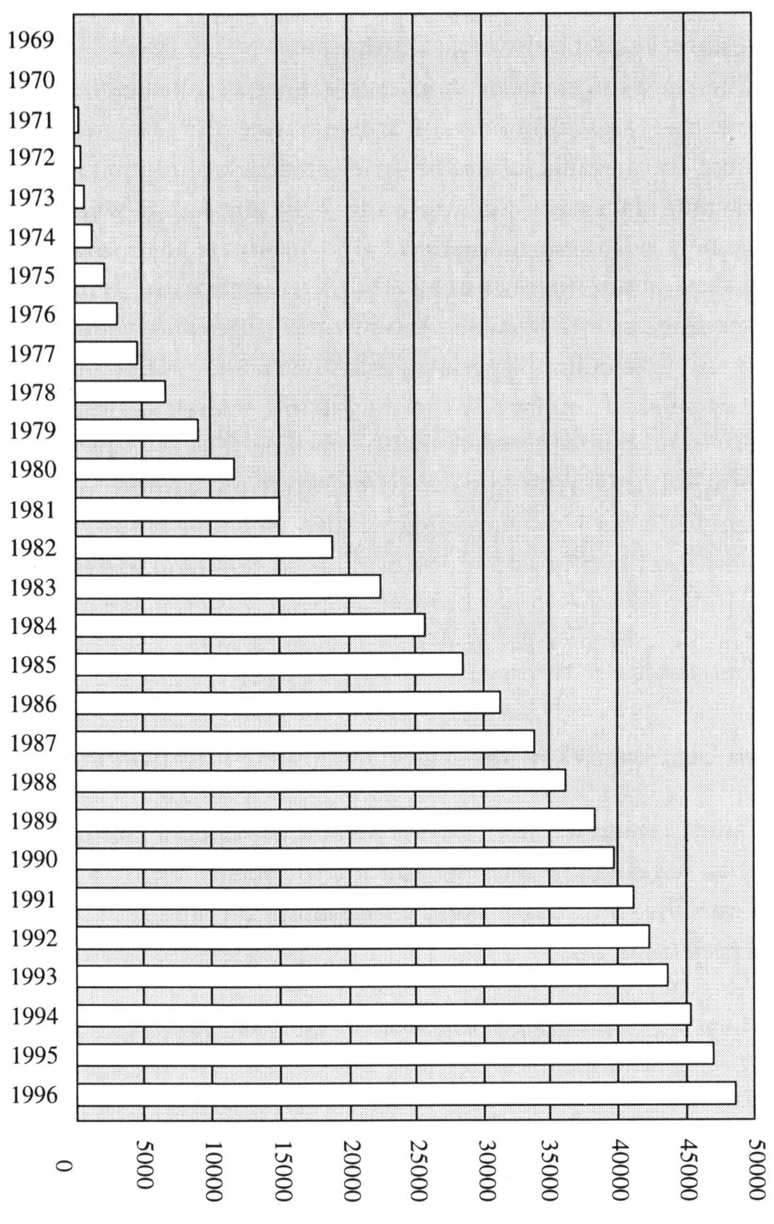

Source: *Konbini '97*, Spring issue, page 26
Note: These statistics seem to include estimated values.

as "uncooked vegetable salad served in a small plastic container" co-developed with Q.P. Corp. and "Calpis water" co-developed with the Calpis Food Industry Co., Ltd.

The latest information about customers was collected by its chain stores: the large numbers of convenience industry were quite valuable for manufacturers. In order to develop popular products, many manufacturers tied up with 7-Eleven Japan which could exclusively sell these newly developed products at its chain stores and thus made the concept of differentiation from other convenience stores possible. As both the seller and manufacturer, 7-Eleven Japan enjoyed special merits thus "co-development" became very popular. Therefore, 7-Eleven Japan's ability to develop new products became unrivaled in the market. Thus, 7-Eleven Japan developed this strategy of differentiation armed with POS information and used it against the negative change of the "intensification of competition with rival companies". It is quite surprising that the POS information from 7-Eleven Japan became very influential as it decided the destiny of major manufacturers.

Two Big Features of the Third Integrated Information System

The third integrated information system provided a computer with graphic information analysis and an interactive POS in order to deal with the "individualization of consumption" and "intensification of competition".

(A) Computer with graphic information analyzing function

In order to let member stores utilize the information system more often and more effectively, 7-Eleven Japan decided to introduce a personal computer with the specific function of displaying data in graphic form. This computer could indicate the following 11 data items on the screen.

Table 2-8. Third integrated information system

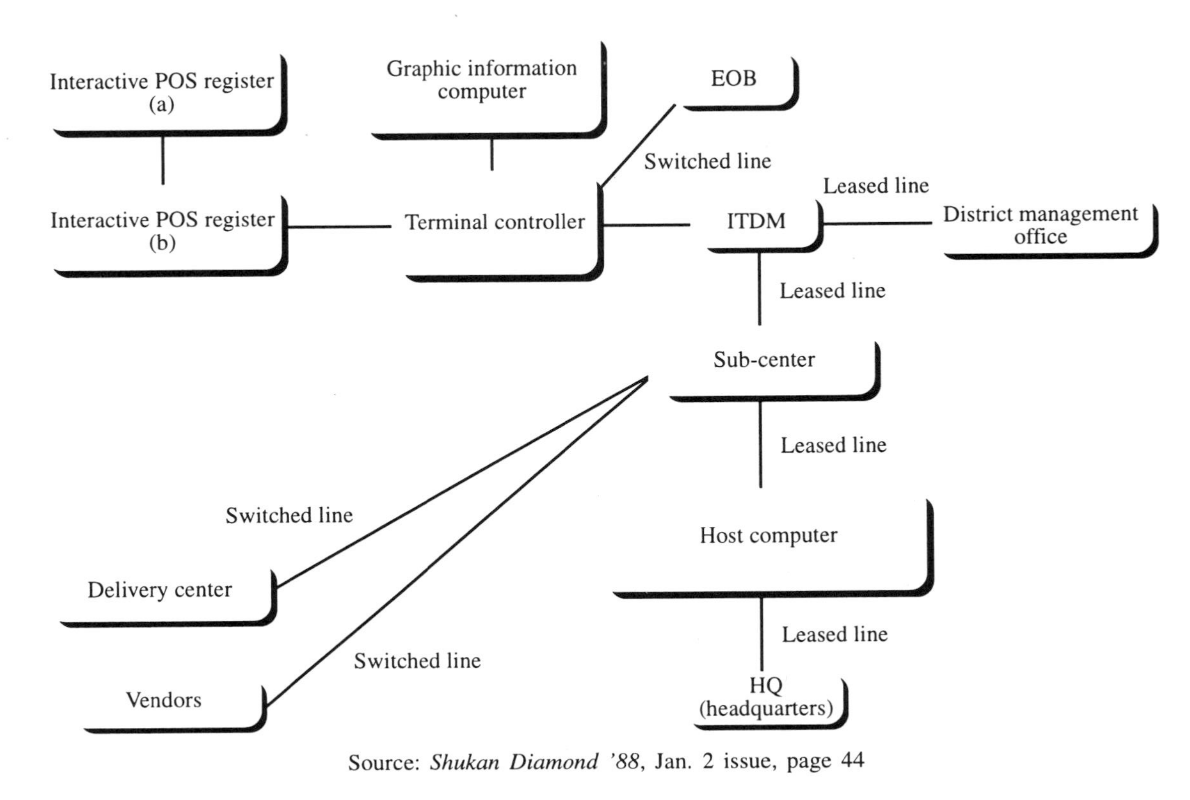

Source: *Shukan Diamond '88*, Jan. 2 issue, page 44

1. List of the sold-out time of daily merchandise.
2. List of sales performance per customer base and time zone of day.
3. Analytical information on disposed merchandise.
4. Sales per single item during 10 days.
5. Information of sales of single items per day and per time zone.
6. Sales analysis per categorized information and daily time zone of day.
7. Analysis of single item per categorized information.
8. Chart of poor-selling merchandise per categorized information.
9. Changes of transactions during 10-week period.
10. Information of magazine sales.
11. Changes in business performance.

Note: 7-Eleven Japan classifies merchandise into PMA and information categories with divisions of single items.

From the above function the headquarters can grasp the following basic information for every member store:

1. What type of customers purchased the merchandise
2. When did they purchase
3. How many products did they purchase

A computer with the function of graphic information analysis plays a very important and central role of "item-by-item management" of 7-Eleven Japan.

(B) Interactive POS register

An interactive register has a 5-inch picture tube and consists of the main register and sub-register. The main register is connected to the terminal controller (TC). As the main register memorizes the selling price per product, queries to TC about the selling price are not required, unlike before. Therefore, the whole process has sped up. Even in times of problem with the TC, the main register can handle the problem. When the main register has problems, a sub-register can carry out the registration works by simply connecting itself to the TC. This system provided the function of risk-decentralization.

Direct access to the host computer with the operation boards of a register was a key technological progression because the display of information from a host computer inquired by a member store on the screen of the register machine became available. Therefore it became possible to perform interactive communications with the register machine.

Furthermore, the collection of detailed information on customers by using the POS register became possible as customer bases were subdivided as follows. This customer information collected by POS plays a key role in the development of new products.

Category of customer bases

Children (male/female)	Below 12 years old
Junior and high school students (male/female)	13–18 years old
Young people (male/female)	19–29 years old
Middle aged (male/female)	30–49 years old
Mature aged (male/female)	Over 50 years old

7-Eleven Japan holds a leading position in the joint development of merchandise with manufacturers because of the richness of this POS information. It is no exaggeration to say that POS information played a huge role in changing the position of the relationship of 7-Eleven Japan and manufacturers.

(C) EOB

New items, the number of sales per single item in the previous week, and the growth rate were added to the order screen and the display of daily food such as rice products, the order volume of cooked bread from the previous day, also became available. As member stores effectively utilized this information, the accuracy of order placement improved.

7-Eleven Japan started to tackle the distribution system when the third integrated information system was introduced. It loaned out its vendor terminals, POS label printer and sorting machines. 7-Eleven Japan has built up an effective distribution system with vendors, who although were external companies, were hooked up via its information system. This is the secret why it can perform highly accurate delivery schedules by treating external companies on a strong trust basis.

Intra-company Innovation Utilizing "Technological Progress"

By the end of 1989, the total number of 7-Eleven Japan member stores had reached nearly 4,000. 7-Eleven Japan received a huge amount of order information. Furthermore, by using the information service, a service of payment acceptance of public utility bills among others, had been rapidly expanding. As the third integrated information system used telephone lines, the capacity of this line had reached its limit. Actually, most of the POS information was sent to the headquarters by floppy disc, not by an on-line method and this caused a one-week delay until such information was available for use. As an information system "in times of rapid changes", this system was obviously deficient in processing speed. Therefore, 7-Eleven Japan started to seek a new system that could handle all information real-time on line.

By the latter half of the 1980s, ISDN lines capable of handling a huge volume of data at high speed became available and 7-Eleven Japan quickly decided to adopt this "technological progress". 7-Eleven Japan built its fourth integrated information system in 1990. By using the ISDN line, the rapid transmission of POS information at the store on-line to the headquarters became possible. In this way, POS data became available at the store and the headquarters only one day after transmission. By referring to POS data, the accuracy of order placement has improved and thus the headquarters could make quicker decisions.

7-Eleven Japan has built up a stronger information system by utilizing "technological progress" provided by ISDN line prior to other competitors. This clearly shows its excellent foresight and progressive spirit.

Cultivation of New Customer Bases by the Information System

The fourth integrated information system contributed not only higher efficiency in order placement and in the development of new products. It also helped to create a service for payment acceptance of electric bills issued by the Tokyo Electric Co.'s other "service based business". Utilizing the information system expanded further after the introduction of the fourth integrated information system capable of handling huge amounts of information. It developed new "service business" such as the payment acceptance of mail order, catalogue shopping, etc. 7-Eleven Japan's store was previously simply a "place to sell merchandise" but now it has became a "place to offer services" as well.

Since the relaxation of operation rules under the auspices of the Large Scale Retail Store Law of 1994, many large-scale retailers extended their business hours, and are now even open on New Year's Day. Therefore the advantage of the convenience industry to "offer time convenience" has begun to be eroded, meaning intensified competition with other categories of business. 7-Eleven Japan has successfully attracted customers and cultivated new customer bases by converting the store to the place of "selling merchandise and offering service". In the midst of intensified competition, the role of the 7-Eleven Japan information system in "creating new business" continues to get bigger and more important.

The Fourth Integrated Information System Connected by ISDN Line

As we discussed in the previous chapter, the fourth integrated information system introduced in the 1990s used an ISDN network. The ordering terminal has changed from the EOB to the GOT (graphic order terminal). The ST (scanner terminal) was developed as an inspection terminal. It was upgraded to have more capability in comparison with an interactive POS system.

In 1992, the information system at the 7-Eleven Japan headquarters was re-built with the client-server system consisting of the host computer, the database server and the work station. Therefore, the POS data of all member stores could be used at the headquarters just after one day of processing through the system. It also became possible to share information within the headquarters with all the departments concerned. The fourth information system consisted of the following features.

A. Store Computer (SC)

The SC is the computer of the entire system that is used in the store and comes with a display unit. It can display on screen all the previous day's information collected from member stores. The contents displayed include:

1. The sales performance for each customer base and per time zone of day.
2. The changes in sales figures of single items in a 10-day period.
3. Sales of single items per day and per time zone of day.
4. Sales statistics of new products.
5. Analysis of disposed products.
6. Assortment evaluation.
7. Sales analysis per categorized information and per time zone.
8. Single item analysis per categorized information.
9. Sales analysis per categorized information.

10. Changes in 10-day transaction period.
11. Information on sales growth rate per categorized information.
12. Analysis of the numbers of shoppers.
13. Analysis of the contribution of gondola sales.

As AI (artificial intelligence) is built into the computer, a real time upgrade of information is possible. Apart from this, it is possible to simultaneously manage order placement and also the surveillance of in-store facilities and equipment. The transmission of data to and from the computer is done by the SC.

B. Graphic Order Terminal (GOT)

GOT is an A4-size electronic book order terminal and has a wider LC screen in comparison with the EOB and it is very bright. When an employee carries out an order placement, information such as the price of the product, the number of delivery vans, and past sales information is clearly indicated on the screen. Some of the data can be shown graphically. In addition, information on new products, trends experienced at other stores and weather information are also easily available. GOT is a tool for unifying the procedure of order placement and providing efficient store information to improve the accuracy of the process of ordering.

C. Scanner Terminal (ST)

This tool is designed to check whether products ordered have been delivered or not and delivery data collected in the in-store computer is updated at the counter. The latest data is available on the computer display of the GOT. An upgraded POS system made it possible to indicate on the screen the number of products delivered, inventory volume, date when the products were sold out, in addition to the quantity of unsold products.

As it can read the position of the product's display as the number of the shelf, shelf number data also became available as an indication.

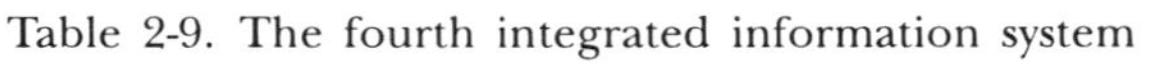

Table 2-9. The fourth integrated information system

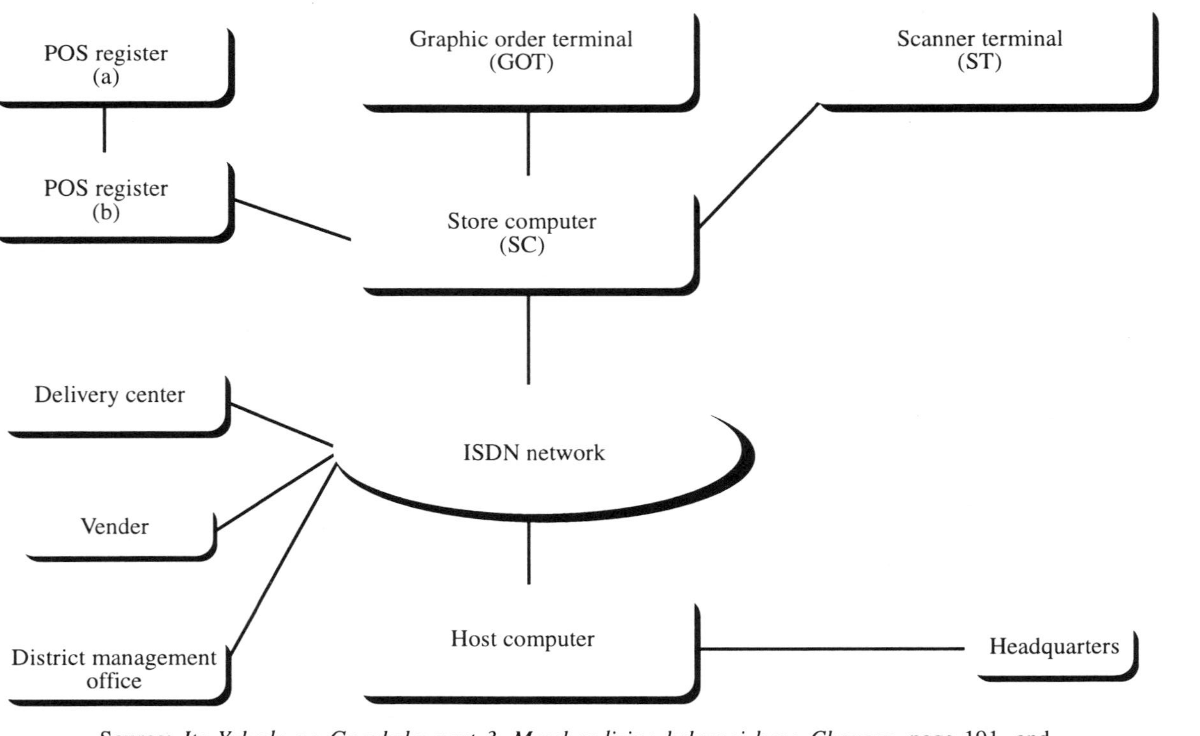

Source: *Ito-Yokado no Gyoukaku part 3*, *Merchandising kakumei heno Chousen*, page 191, and *7-Eleven no Jouhou Kakumei*, page 183

D. An Interactive POS Register

The processing capacity has increased 5-fold compared with conventional process capacity, thanks to a high performance computer present in the register. In addition, the 9-inch screen is visible to both the customer and the register and a high-speed printer was installed. This enabled the store to show information from the host computer to a customer. Furthermore, the printing time was drastically shortened and the high-speed transmission of huge volume of information to the host computer became possible due to the connection with an ISDN line.

At the end of the 1980's, a "manpower shortage" became a serious problem and had a serious impact on the store's management. 7-Eleven Japan hired many part-time workers at its stores all over Japan. Therefore, its immediate task was to make them into productive employees despite their lack of experience. The fourth integrated information system was designed based on the concept that "anybody can use it". While 7-Eleven Japan has been pursuing high sophistication in information systems of high speed, it should not be forgotten that it also attached vital importance to the concept of "ease of operation". The technology was a great success only through unification of "information systems and people", that is to say, the "hardware and software".

Chapter 3

Secrets of 7-Eleven Japan's Excellent Ability in New Product Development

Quick Recognition of the Arrival of More "Value-Oriented Times"

After the collapse of the bubble economy, many sections of the retail industry could not correctly anticipate changing customer needs. During the bubble economy, consumers sought after the cheapness of a product rather than quality concerns. As it was then quite a prosperous time, the trend was that consumers purchased cheaper type products which were quickly used, disposed and replaced. Stores selling men's suit at cut-price rates had been quite popular and this symbolized the price- rather than quality-oriented times.

However, in 1990, the tastes of consumers started to change and they began to place more importance on value for money as consumer's income declined or stagnated. Consumers started to shop more carefully and selected products based on value and quality rather than merely the selling price. Consequently, the numbers of heavy selling product lines experienced limited growth. Supermarkets who did not grasp the change in consumption patterns to more value-oriented times suffered from poor sales. This was because they stuck to a strategy of bargain sales which were so popular during the bubble economy. 7-Eleven Japan quickly recognized the arrival of these value-oriented times and made a pinpoint selection of products and quantities to sell at each store. Thus, 7-Eleven Japan adapted to the change of the time by offering good value and higher quality products to customers.

How again could 7-Eleven Japan notice the change in the needs of consumers prior to competitors? The reason was that 7-Eleven Japan had the most advanced information system in the retail industry and closely monitored the change of consumer sentiments by using POS in real-time analysis. Also 7-Eleven Japan possessed an organizational climate that allowed it to grasp and convert the change to a business chance, a quick response to the change of the times.

Table 3-1. Ratio of fast food accounting for the sales of the industry

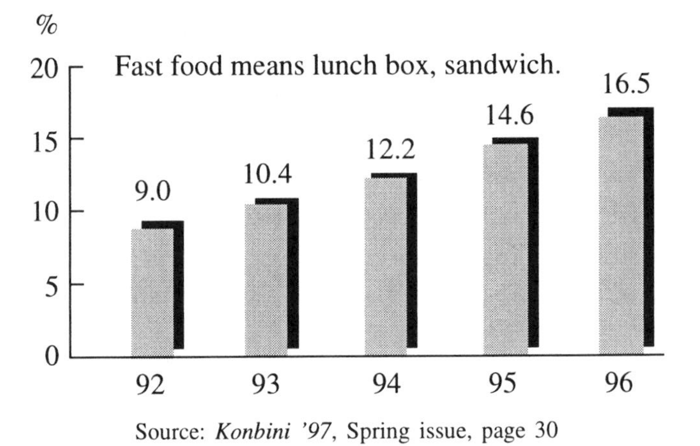

Source: *Konbini '97*, Spring issue, page 30

The Lunch-Box: 7-Eleven Japan's Vital Strategic Product

Lunch boxes are very strategic products for all convenience stores, as each convenience store can easily differentiate itself from competitors in the battle to attract more customers. According to MCR statistics, fast food (lunch box, sandwiches) account for 16.5% of the total convenience store sales in 1996 and this percentage has been steadily increasing. 7-Eleven Japan sells more than 200 million lunch box sets every year. We can interpret its careful strategy in terms of the product development, sales and distribution.

7-Eleven Japan does not possess its own production facilities and makes it a policy to form joint development deals with vendors. 7-Eleven Japan has a strong influence over vendors in guiding the type of product the vendors actually produce. This is called an alliance of production and sales systems. As most vendors are small- and medium-sized, there were only a few vendors who could satisfy the standards required by 7-Eleven Japan. Therefore, it urged vendors to organize themselves into the Japan Delicatessen Food Cooperative Society so that vendors could jointly grapple with the key issues of the improvement of production facilities, quality control and distribution. At first, vendors resisted opening their know-how to other competitors, but later they agreed to cooperate. As a result of this, the vendors enjoyed the advantage of their products being sold extensively at 7-Eleven Japan stores.

Co-Development with Manufacturers with 7-Eleven Japan Taking the Leadership Role

7-Eleven Japan also co-developed new products with major food manufacturers. This method is called co-development or team merchandise. Co-development has some major advantages for 7-Eleven Japan and the manufacturers. The advantages for the manufacturers are:

1. Manufacturers' products are sold extensively in the approximately 7,000 chain stores of 7-Eleven Japan spread all over the country.
2. Results of product marketing are collectable using the POS system.
3. Crucial data of consumers and market which are indispensable for future development of their products are obtainable.

At the same time the advantages that 7-Eleven Japan enjoy are:

1. For a period of time, 7-Eleven Japan can sell those newly developed products on an exclusive basis allowing differentiation from competitors.
2. Obtain information from manufacturers prior to other competitors.

The most noticeable point is that co-development is carried out under the leadership of 7-Eleven Japan. Therefore, most manufacturers do not have direct contact with customers. At times when the preference of consumers is changing rapidly, it is natural that products developed solely by manufacturers are not best suited to satisfy the needs of consumers. In order to develop high-selling products, real time consumer information is quite indispensable and this data is hard for manufacturers to obtain. In order to achieve this, the POS information available from 7-Eleven Japan is the knowledge that manufacturers want to gather at all costs. This is the reason why 7-Eleven Japan can hold a leading position in co-development. It is a symbol of the times of rapid change that POS information brought about a reversal in the previously manufacturer dominant relationship.

Offering a New Service and Expanding Business

Parcel home-delivery, color copying, catered lunch boxes ordered in advance, and the printing of New Year cards are some of the diverse new services offered by 7-Eleven Japan which has introduced a constant stream of new services since the 1980's. The most frequently used service is the payment acceptance service for public utility charges. 7-Eleven Japan registered 38,000 transactions of this service amounting to 275 billion yen in 1996. It is quite surprising to see that the volume of this service transaction in the entire convenience industry has reached 1 trillion yen. In addition to public utility charges, 7-Eleven Japan provides the service of payment acceptance for mail-order sales, life insurance and casualty insurance. Furthermore, customers can settle payment by credit card. Thus the element of "convenience" has been steadily rising.

7-Eleven Japan has been developing these new services to match customer's potential needs. Thus, the diversification of services will help expand the customer base and bring about "incidental shopping". 7-Eleven Japan did not accept that the store was merely a "place to sell merchandise", but it understood that it was also a "place to offer services". This way of thinking gave birth to a succession of new services.

POS Playing a Central Role in 7-Eleven Japan's Strategy

There is no end of possibilities in the development of new products for 7-Eleven Japan which established business links with Dig Cube Inc., and specialized in the sale of software in convenience stores. 7-Eleven Japan started the sales of game software from November 1996 and sold game software equivalent to 12 billion yen by March 1997, a period of less than 6 months due to the big sales of the "Final Fantasy 7" game.

The parent company of Dig Cube is Square, who is a major software maker. Square distributed its products through wholesale stores and had always been suffering in the decision-making process regarding forecasting the exact production quantity, as sales estimates of wholesale stores were not reliable. Since the major product was a cassette-type software that took one or two months for production, Square could not respond promptly to additional orders. Therefore, there was no other option but to produce on an estimated basis which is a risky production method.

However, Sony Computer Entertainment Ltd. begun to sell Play Station on a CD-ROM drive that is possible to produce in just one week after receiving orders. Square, therefore, decided to switch its production system to supply CD-ROM type software, which is produced and delivered in a shorter period after receiving orders. It made efforts to break free from production based on estimates and decided to sell its products via distribution channels other than wholesale stores. Square proposed a sales cooperation deal to several convenience stores. Of course 7-Eleven Japan with its highly evaluated POS system was included in this proposal for sales cooperation.

7-Eleven Japan accepted the proposal from Square because this business link enabled the development of new customer bases and allowed the sale of products with higher unit prices. After this business link with 7-Eleven Japan, Square could access POS information and this had the great merit of minimizing the inventory volume and stock short-out problems. This is a successful example of the development of a new product "alliance" that generates merits for both parties. We should not overlook the key role that 7-Eleven Japan's POS information system played in connecting the strategy of both companies.

Grasping Trends of "Deregulation" and "New Product Development"

"Deregulation" has already started in many areas. For example, the sales of stamps, postcards, and revenue stamps became possible at convenience stores in 1996. 7-Eleven Japan recorded sales figures equivalent to 9 billion yen in this area in 1996. Stamps and other products that customers frequently request contribute to increased store loyalty from customers even though the products themselves have low profit margins. In 1997 deregulation occurred in the travel industry. In 1998, the medical supplies and finance industries were deregulated and many other areas will also be affected. We will discuss in the next chapter how 7-Eleven Japan copes with deregulation, a key of the trend of the times.

Table 3-2. Integrated system of production, distribution, and sales of ice cream

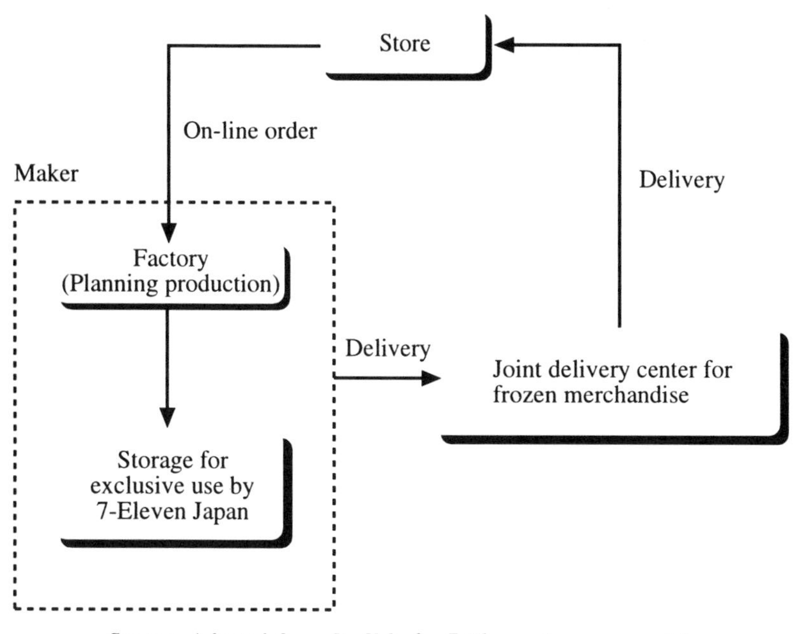

Source: Adapted from *Ito-Yokado, 7-Eleven Japan*, page 98

Selling Summer Products in the Winter Season

7-Eleven Japan invested approximately 4 billion yen in the construction of large-sized refrigeration boxes for ice cream in 1994 and installed them in all of its chain stores. It is quite natural that ice cream sells well in summer time. However, 7-Eleven Japan predicted that even in winter, ice cream would sell well as home heating facilities had improved. As a result in 1994, 7-Eleven Japan recorded more than a two-fold increase in ice cream sales in comparison with the previous year. The refrigeration box was placed in the center of the store where five gondolas used to be stationed. This was a drastic and innovative use of space as convenience stores have a limited space.

Morinaga Milk Industry Co., Ltd, Morinaga and Company Ltd, Snow Brand Milk Products Co., Ltd, Akagi Nyugyo, and Hagen Daas were the main suppliers. Until then, ice cream was mainly produced in the winter season and prepared for the concentration of sales in summer. However, manufacturers were unable to respond quickly to the change in the market. It was not possible to increase the production of popular ice cream because it would only build up inventory volume. Therefore, 7-Eleven Japan established a system to sell ice cream within 10 days after placing orders. The features of the system are as follows:

— On-line transmission of order information and inventory volume of the store directly to producers.
— Manufacturers produce based on this information and store them in a storage facility especially prepared for 7-Eleven Japan.
— The exact quantity required is delivered to the joint delivery center for frozen products.
— From this center, products are delivered to the stores.

In this way, 7-Eleven Japan has constructed a consistent production, distribution, and sales system for ice cream products. Thus, it became possible for the store to sell very fresh ice cream throughout the year. In addition, 7-Eleven Japan tied up with Morinaga Milk Industry Co., Ltd, Morinaga Company, Ltd and Akagi Nyugyou for the development of new products and has developed new types of ice cream that satisfied customers' needs. This is an excellent reflection of 7-Eleven Japan's attitude towards "taste" and "freshness". 7-Eleven Japan attaches importance to the "un-learning effect", something that breaks away from the existing concept. This is why it could carry out a very drastic innovation in order to sell "summer products during the winter season".

A New Strategic Weapon of the Convenience Store, the Multimedia Station (MMS)

The multimedia station (MMS) is a terminal that enables sales of mail order and travel commodities, ticket reservations, the rewriting of game software and is connected with collaborating companies. Customers operate the system by using the data display for making their reservations, etc. Credit card payment or cashing services are also available at some MMS.

The biggest advantages are that MMS can offer various kinds of merchandise and services only with this equipment. Although there are several other convenience chains offering ticket reservation service, etc., this usually causes congestion problems at the counter. As MMS is not installed at the counter, the congestion can be minimized.

Lawson, Family Mart, Sunkist, and Mini Top have already started to introduce MMS. New products such as discount package tours, and products that are usually difficult to locate elsewhere are hot-selling items in MMS. Among the contents of MMS, the function of rewriting of game software for video games, available at Lawson, is quite epoch-breaking. By inserting memory cassettes into the MMS, it performs a rewriting to a new software of what the customer wishes. The time required for rewriting is approximately three minutes even with a capacity of 32 MB.

Due to this, the delivery of software and inventory is no longer required. This software product has one of the highest unit prices among merchandise sold in the store and contributes healthily to the sales of the store. Each store tries to offer its own unique uses of MMS. Sunkist offers horoscopes, applications for compulsory car inspections and nursing information. Mini-top accepts order of fast food with MMS in order to minimize the congestion at the counter. MMS has much potential in the ability to develop diversification of products and services in the narrow and limited space of the store. In these times of increasing deregulation, the various services offered by MMS are becoming indispensable. However, 7-Eleven Japan, despite always being in the pioneering position in the retail industry, has not yet installed MMS terminal as of 1997. How 7-Eleven Japan will respond to this big change will be watched with keen interest with the arrival of the multimedia age.

Table 3-3. Concept of Lawson's MMS system

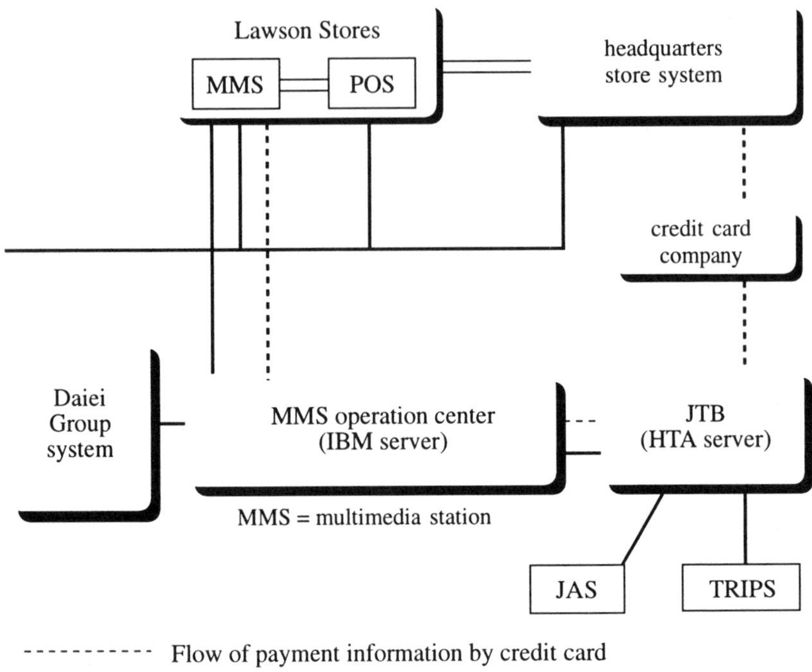

Source: Adapted from *Nikkei Trends '97*, December issue, page 23

Chapter 4

The Innovative Distribution System of 7-Eleven Japan

Distribution Cost Saving by Using the "Dominant System"

7-Eleven Japan does not operate chain stores in Aomori Prefecture, Aichi Prefecture, Okayama Prefecture, or Nagasaki Prefectures. To be precise, as Table 4-1 shows, 7-Eleven Japan has opened its stores in only 24 out of 47 administrative divisions in Japan. Why has 7-Eleven Japan not opened stores in many prefectures when it has the largest numbers of chain stores in the convenience industry?

Since convenience chains are not producers, they purchase products from manufacturers and sell them at the stores. There is not such a big difference in purchase costs. Distribution costs account for nearly 10% of the purchase costs and, this area is a key factor in differentiating profitability. Therefore, it is an important task for convenience stores to strive to cut down distribution costs. Since its establishment, 7-Eleven Japan has based its strategy on a method called the "dominant system": meaning focusing operations in certain areas which are then crowded with multiple stores. Therefore, there are many prefectures where 7-Eleven Japan's convenience stores have not opened. As stores are crowded into narrow areas, distribution costs can be minimized because long distance delivery by vendors is not required. Time required for delivery can also be shortened. There is an additional advantage in the "dominant system" besides the above. One of the key elements

Table 4-1. Number of 7-Eleven Japan stores for every prefecture

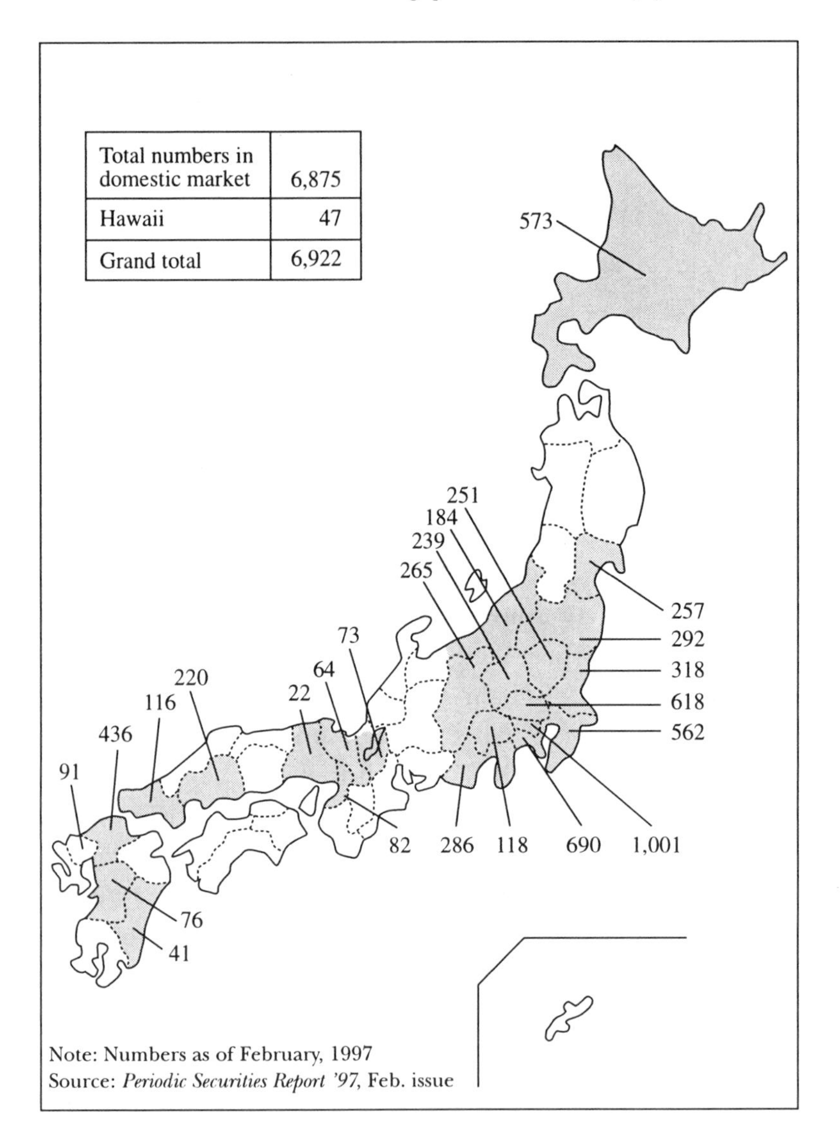

Total numbers in domestic market	6,875
Hawaii	47
Grand total	6,922

Note: Numbers as of February, 1997
Source: *Periodic Securities Report* '97, Feb. issue

affecting a store's overall sales comes from TV commercials. Although huge advertisement expenses would be required to broadcast commercials all over Japan, 7-Eleven Japan spends less as the covered area is quite limited. Furthermore, as the area coverage is limited the OFC can go around the stores more often giving crucial advice on store management.

7-Eleven Japan's first outlet was opened in the Koto Ward and the second was under its direct management in Sagamihara city. In the Tokyo area, 7-Eleven Japan has concentrated in the Koto Ward. Since its establishment, 7-Eleven Japan has never changed its strategy of opening stores using this "dominant system". A strong management attitude to keep this basic concept underlies the present-day status of 7-Eleven Japan. On the contrary, Lawson has developed its strategy to open stores all over Japan, in complete contrast with the strategy of 7-Eleven Japan. We are always surprised with the foresight of 7-Eleven Japan who understands the importance of the distribution system.

The Distribution Revolution Begins with the Intensified Use of Wholesale Agents

Until the first half of the 1970s when Japan had enjoyed a continuous and high economic growth, manufacturers had been dominating retailers. Since the market norm was actually a shortage of products, producers held a strong position in the market. They developed products and had affiliated agents who distributed their products. There were many cases when retailers very often could not get what they wanted to purchase. 7-Eleven Japan wanted to be recognized as the company who provided the convenience of one-stop shopping: you can find all the products you want to buy in the store. For this purpose, 7-Eleven Japan had to create a system of small lot delivery and high frequency delivery.

7-Eleven Japan started to tackle this challenge with an innovative transformation of the manufacturer-driven logistic system. It restructured the logistic system to a system of appointed agents responsible for each particular delivery. Therefore, the logistic system handled only the delivery of merchandise produced by multiple

Table 4-2. Intensive delivery system of 7-Eleven Japan

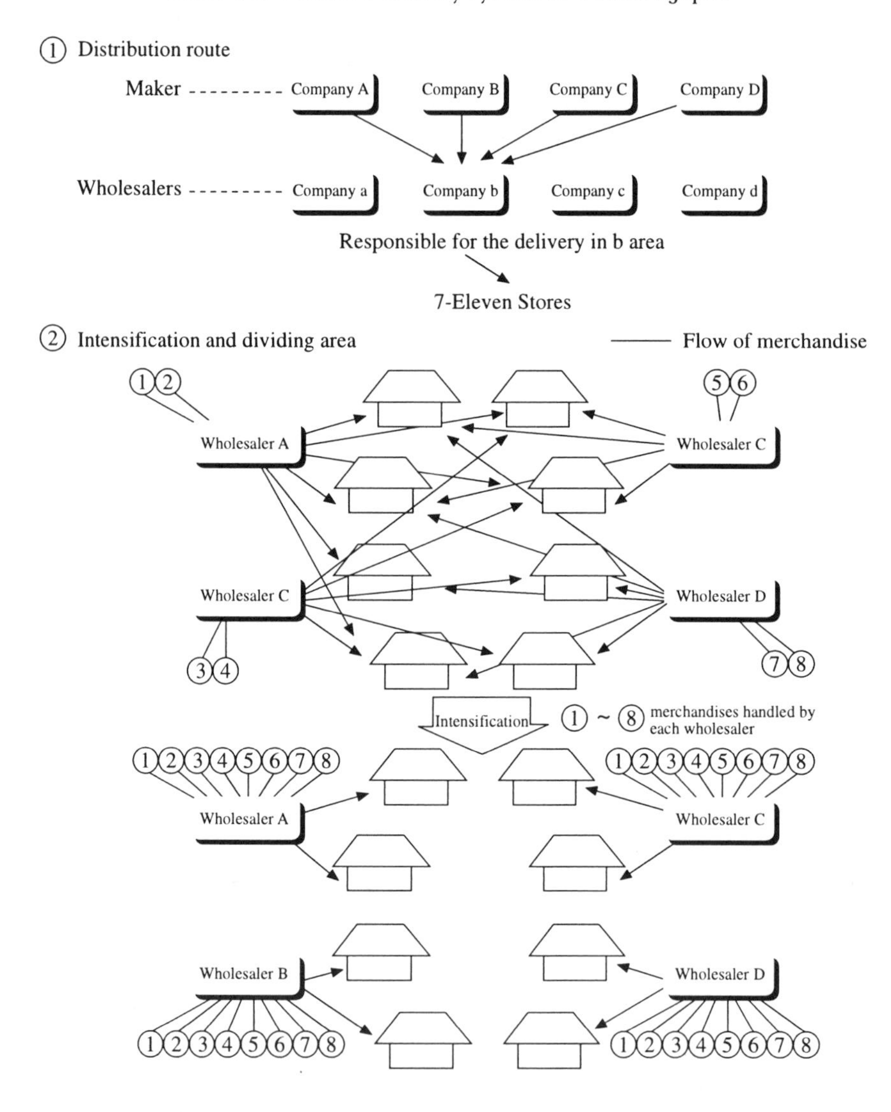

Source: *A Beginners' Course on Distribution*, page 251

Table 4-3. Joint delivery system of 7-Eleven Japan

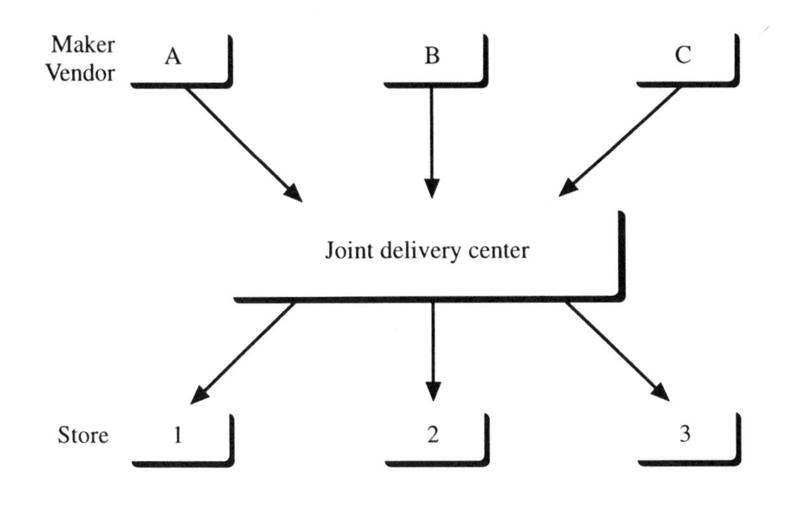

Table 4-4. Number of delivery vans used per day per store

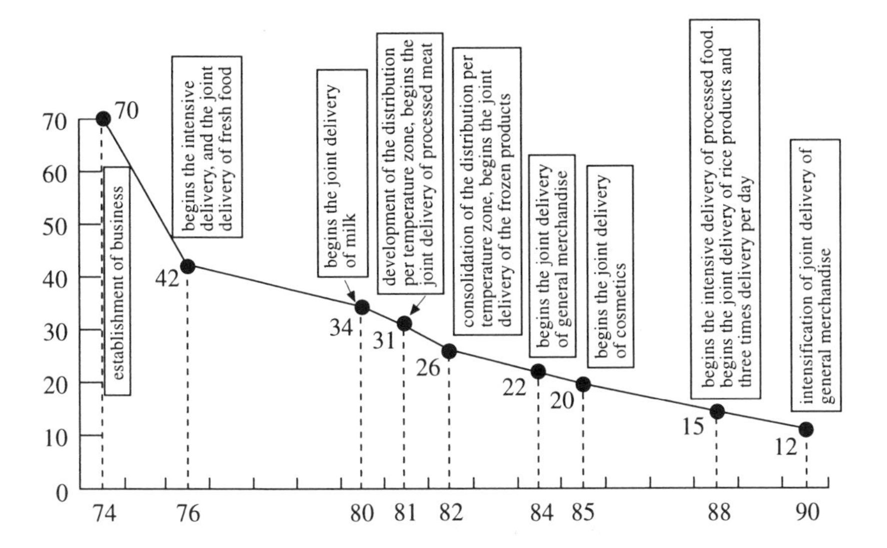

makers. This is what is called the logistic system of "intensive delivery" and it had the following advantages:

1. It is possible to shorten the delivery distance and time.
2. Reduction of the number of delivery vans.
3. Delivery volume to the store per delivery increases and the efficiency of the loading capacity improves.

7-Eleven Japan emphasized the advantages generated by the intensive delivery system and requested the cooperation of agents. However, at the initial stage, 7-Eleven Japan encountered opposition from many quarters as this new delivery system meant the destruction of the existing delivery system. However, agents eventually accepted 7-Eleven Japan's reasonable way of thinking and strong passion for the new delivery system.

Maintaining the Taste and Freshness of Foodstuff

In order to keep the taste and freshness of foodstuff at the highest level, an appropriate temperature for all foodstuff must be maintained during delivery. 7-Eleven Japan classifies four different product types, i.e., frozen, refrigerated, normal temperature, and insulated foodstuffs. Since the lunch box is a key strategic product, 7-Eleven Japan takes into close consideration the best method of delivery. In order to maintain freshness, a variety of lunch boxes are delivered by a special delivery van with an internal temperature unit of 20 degrees. Both in mid-summer and mid-winter, the delivery van with both cooling and heating functions keeps a constant 20-degree temperature. As the type of lunch box will differ depending on the time zone of the day, 7-Eleven Japan schedules three deliveries in a day: morning delivery, mid-day delivery, and evening delivery to deliver lunch boxes that meet the customer's needs.

7-Eleven Japan has even delivered lunch boxes by using helicopters and motorbikes at times when roads were blocked due to a natural disaster or simply bad traffic jams, overlooking profit concerns on these occasions. This shows that its attitude in taking good care of customers is strong. 7-Eleven Japan is particular about the thorough management of freshness and good taste as a tool to differentiate its merchandise from that of other competitors. The role of this distribution system will get bigger and bigger as competition with its peers becomes more intensified.

Information System Supporting Logistic Strategy

The logistics system of 7-Eleven Japan would not be functional without the integrated information system. Orders from member stores come at 10:00 a.m. one day before delivery. However, lunch box orders, which are delivered three times daily, can be accepted by 10:00 a.m. and be delivered later that evening. Order information is sent via ISDN network to the host computer at the headquarters. Order information is automatically transmitted between 10:45 a.m. and noon to the manufacturers and agents regarding the delivery instruction. According to the delivery instruction, manufacturers will prepare products and deliver them to the joint delivery center.

Between noon and 13:00 p.m., delivery statements per maker, shipment statement per store and delivery slips of each delivery are sent from the host computer to the joint delivery center. Delivered merchandise will be sorted out for each store in accordance with the shipment statement. Products are loaded onto the delivery van, according to the order of delivery to stores. In this way, the time required for delivery work is minimized drastically. 7-Eleven Japan's delivery system is strongly characterized by the information system with a systematic integration of orders, manufacturing and delivery. The "information system", "joint delivery system" and "dominant strategy" supports the incomparable logistic system of 7-Eleven Japan.

Unifying the Delivery of Liquor and Processed Food

Taking into consideration deregulation in the area of liquor sales and processed food, 7-Eleven Japan is planning to establish a company handling the comprehensive delivery of liquor and processed food on an exclusive basis. In the meantime, the H.I. Corp. will be established with a joint investment by Hokushu Ren, Itochu Corp., and Itochu Food Co. This company will deliver liquor and processed food in the entire Hokkaido area. Merchandise will be delivered to member stores from the delivery center located in five different places in Hokkaido. Later, this new company wants to expand a similar distribution company all over Japan, in order to cater for the increasing number of stores where liquor is handled. Since the same delivery van will deliver those products, loading efficiency will be drastically improved. This company specializing in the distribution will be fully equipped with a computer system for preparing the database of traffic and road information to achieve the improvement of efficiency of delivery works.

Establishment of a Distribution Base in Taiwan to Unify the Overseas Distribution System

7-Eleven Japan is also tackling the task of improving the distribution of merchandise imported into Japan. Merchandise for daily use by 7-Eleven Japan and produced in Asian countries have been delivered by producers directly to Tokyo Bay and thereafter delivered to stores all over Japan. This delivery system requires long distance domestic transportation generating higher delivery costs. 7-Eleven Japan is planning to tie up with a Taiwanese shipping company group, Choei, to prepare a distribution base in an area located in the city center of Taichung. All merchandise produced in Asian countries will be gathered here and, based on order information from Japan via the internet, will then be shipped to 10 different seaports in Japan. Thus, distribution costs will be drastically minimized. Since its establishment, 7-Eleven Japan has had a strong and higher motivation to have an efficient distribution system. It is presumed that the implementation of distribution systems with a global perspective will be further developed in the future.

Chapter 5

Analyzing the Robustness of 7-Eleven Japan According to Personality and Organization

The Management Philosophy of Hirofumi Suzuki, the Virtual Founder of 7-Eleven Japan

When we talk about the "personality" of 7-Eleven Japan, we should not forget Hirofumi Suzuki, who is virtually a founder of 7-Eleven Japan, and still an acting commander of the company as its Chairman. Suzuki graduated from Chuo University and worked at Tohan Corp. for a while before taking up employment at Ito-Yokado Co., Ltd. in 1963. He was assigned to the management department despite not having any sales experience. This is perhaps the reason why his career is seen as quite unique. Suzuki negotiated with Southland Ltd., USA to realize the tie-up with Ito-Yokado and then took the lead in the management of 7-Eleven Japan from its establishment to the present day.

We will find the essence of the management philosophy of 7-Eleven Japan in a collection of his sayings. He repeatedly says that the basis of the management is a "response to change" and "self-reformation". It is very interesting that he insists upon a top-down decision-making system, while the efficiency of a flat organization is strongly advocated.

1. My management idea is quick response to change under any circumstances.

2. It is important to have the ability to change your way of thinking in order to respond to change.
3. Only through self-reformation can stores and companies conduct their business successfully and in the surest way.
4. To create new business it is important to succeed where others have given up because of lack of business opportunities and thus to break with practical wisdom.
5. Successful experience in the past will not be of any help in the present when the abolishment of the status-quo is required.
6. In business it is necessary to think of what the customer is looking for and what we must do now, without even mentioning the response to change.
7. At the time when so much response to change is required, things could not change without top-down quick decisions.
8. A leader should be self-aware and be able to objectively view his own conduct.
9. Forecasting years ahead and making plans based on it only makes one inflexible to change.

Suzuki considers the concept of a correct order placement based on item-by-item management should be the foundation of the retail business, and understands that POS is the tool to fulfill this function.

1. For the retail business, the most significant thing is to place orders with self-direction.
2. It is always required to formulate a hypothesis, carry out, and inspect the outcome.
3. POS is simply a tool for inspecting the hypothesis formulated.
4. Grasping trends in the sales of single items and inspection with deep analysis of the relation of cause and effect and the background must be carried out.
5. Measures on how to avoid the loss of business opportunities will be directly linked to the business performance.

Suzuki considers the development of differentiation from others, even in the buyer's market, which eliminates unnecessary competition. In addition, he poses a question to the idea of "increasing the assortment of products in compliance with the diversification of consumption" and insists that the narrowing down of products with regard to value is very important.

1. In a buyer's market it is necessary to operate the business from a customer's standpoint.
2. It is very important to be near the customers and feel what they need to be able to fulfill self-differentiation.
3. Much diversification was the product of prejudice by the selfish imagination of manufacturers and sellers.
4. In times of diversification, it is important to narrow down the range to the most sellable products.
5. Inclinations in consumption trends are moving to value-oriented products from price-oriented ones.
6. Without pursuing quality, the attainment of quantitative results cannot be expected.

Suzuki attaches great importance to the utilization of external resources rather than management resources such as employees, facilities, and money. In addition, he considers that management know-how of retail business could not be used unless it is developed in accordance with the climate of the country.

It is quite interesting to see the sharp contrast in the stance between Lawson, who are developing chains all over Japan and that of Suzuki, who believes in the dominant strategy.

1. It is sometimes better and more effective not to hold ownership.
2. The Japanese keiretsu does not necessarily mean the predominance of ownership and holdings but it is very often the case of only the network types with a partial capital participation or no capital relationship at all.

3. Power should not be distributed but should be concentrated.
4. It should be remembered that the retail business is basically a domestic business.
5. The way of thinking that everything should follow the USA model has been prevailing in the distribution industry and does not make any sense.
6. Invest positively in information.
7. Management should be carried out in harmony with balance and adjustment without prejudice.
8. What is most required at the present time is to build up a strategy based on new ways of thinking. Management should not be driven by conventional operations.

(This collection of his quotes were extracted from the books and magazines listed in the Bibliography.)

Another Information Route — Direct Communications

We have repeatedly discussed the superiority of the information system of 7-Eleven Japan in this book. However, the information system is not the only tool of communication to connect the stores and headquarters. 7-Eleven Japan posts operation field counsellors at the rate of 1 to 7 persons to eight of its member stores. The OFC notifies stores of the headquarters' policy and is responsible for playing a very important role in reporting market and member stores' trends back to the headquarters.

The OFC belongs to the district management office with the District Manager (DM) as the head. The Zone Manager (ZM) commanding seven to eight DMs is posted at the headquarters. Every Monday the managerial meeting is attended by HQ management, the directory managers, the zone managers and every Tuesday the OFC meeting is held with attendance of the HQ management and the OFCs from all over Japan. At the OFC meeting, the headquarters policy, new product information, and guidance plans

Table 5-1. Information route by a "person" of 7-Eleven Japan

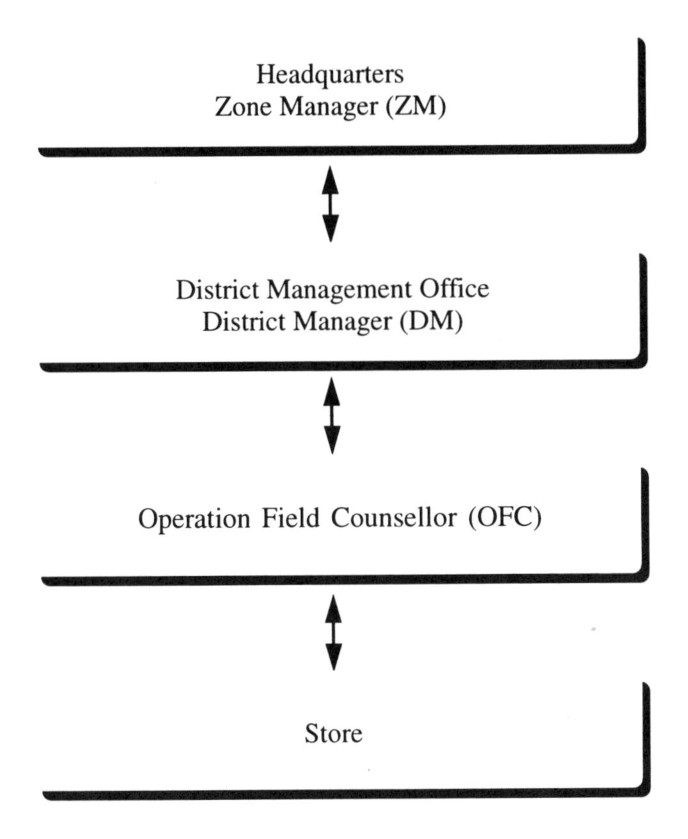

for stores are discussed. Successful cases are reported as all participants share information from the headquarters and stores.

Headquarters use the information collected directly from the OFCs to help build up a coherent strategy. The OFCs in turn quickly pass on HQ policy to member stores. The OFCs conduct ceaseless efforts in providing guidance to member stores on how to make each store more attractive to customers.

7-Eleven Japan holds two management meetings every week as it attaches great importance and value to the direct person-to-person communication method. In fact, estimates are that it spends over 20 billion yen per year on these meetings. Without careful personal guidance, the information system alone is not enough to generate a sense of unity within the organization. 7-Eleven Japan recognizes that it would not be able to conduct a smooth administration of the organization with just this type of information, no matter how excellent the information systems. Therefore, during times of rapid change, it is possible to respond in an appropriate and timely way when combining knowledge provided by the "information system" and from "communication with people".

Basic Concept of Independent Order Placement

When we look at 7-Eleven Japan which is such a strong technological information-oriented organization, many people would assume that it would install an automatic ordering system in each store to make the system even more efficient. However, 7-Eleven Japan strongly rejected this idea. So what is 7-Eleven Japan's future concept of the order placement process? Needless to say, a key factor leading to growth in sales and profits concerns the right assortment of hot-selling products in the store. Therefore, 7-Eleven Japan considers order placement the most important area in retailing.

The first thing member stores must do is to formulate a "hypothesis" of which product, how many and at what time, they should sell the following day? Based on this hypothesis, they fulfill their order placement. Thereafter, they compare actual sales performance with their hypothesis, in order to "inspect" whether their order has been accurate or not. So, 7-Eleven Japan's basic concept of order placement is to help enhance the accuracy of order placement by repeating a process of "hypothesis, fulfillment, and inspection".

Graphic order terminals (GOT) used in the fourth integrated information system are key tools for fulfilling this enhanced accurate ordering goal. As GOT is a handy (A4-size) type terminal, the operator can carry order input work at the place where products are shelved. It is very convenient for operators as they can also see the various POS data such as inventory information, new merchandise information and weather information on the screen of the GOT. However, POS information is past data and it cannot forecast definitely how many and what product would be sellable the next day. Therefore, member store staff need to carry out the management of order placement. It is a "person", not a machine, that can best judge and formulate this self-hypothesis. Obviously customers' needs vary across different member stores. Also member stores, besides the general POS information, can also gather the latest information on events in their surrounding areas and the trends of local rival stores. They utilize this highly relevant information as a useful reference in order placement. 7-Eleven Japan is not interested in issues such as the similar assortment of merchandise for all its chain stores or the introduction of an automatic ordering system. No matter how technically excellent the POS and GOT systems are, they are simply non-reasoning machines. Under steadily changing external surroundings, the decision-making ability of "people" is still the most valued. Therefore 7-Eleven Japan will continue to build its order placement system based on this concept.

Idea of "Co-existence and Co-prosperity" Brings About Robustness

"Co-existence and co-prosperity" with other small- and medium-sized local retailers was one of the central concepts of 7-Eleven Japan during the time of its business establishment. Convenience chains consist of stores under direct management (called training stores) of the headquarters and franchise stores. 7-Eleven Japan focused mainly on the opening of franchise stores in order to avoid misunderstanding with local retailers.

Via this method, 7-Eleven Japan could avoid friction with medium- and small-sized retailers and the opening of new stores was done without causing any major problems. Thus, stores under the franchise system played a major role as a means for small-sized retail stores with poor future prospects in their own business to change their style of business. Stores under the direct management of 7-Eleven Japan make up only 3.4% (231 stores) out of the total number of stores (6,922 stores). Although we cannot make a conclusive judgement as to whether franchise stores are better than stores under direct management, the business performance of franchise stores in general are better than stores under direct management. Since store managers of franchise store are self-employed people who have invested in the store at their own risk, no failure in the business is allowable. Also self-employed store managers often have an entrepreneurial spirit with a strong motivation towards the business. Thus, the higher ratio of franchise stores contribute to higher daily sales amount per store in average.

In addition, the composition of 7-Eleven Japan's stores is characterized by its high ratio of ex-liquor store which converted their business into convenience stores. As selling liquor is possible in these stores, it is natural this adds to the total sales figures. Utilizing this extra profit as a motivating factor, 7-Eleven Japan had been proactively converting liquor stores with good locations into convenience stores prior to competitors. It could be said that generally 7-Eleven Japan is a chain organization composed of stores that produce higher profit margins. The robustness of 7-Eleven Japan does not only originate from the information system, the excellent capability of new product development or the distribution system, but also crucially from the concept of "co-existence and co-prosperity". This concept made it possible to expand the number of franchise stores and create stores that could handle liquor. It clearly shows that the most important elements in being a robust company comprise the "human" and "organization" elements.

Outsourcing Prevents Organization Stiffness

7-Eleven Japan has made positive business use of external sources. For example, when developing food products, it helped to create the "Japan Delicatessen Foods Cooperative Association" for the medium- and small-sized producers. With major manufacturers, 7-Eleven Japan has been positively developing "co-development" and "team merchandising". With vendors, 7-Eleven Japan has organized the "joint delivery" system. Almost all stores are franchised entities run by self-employed persons. Many diverse business connections are united together to share their fate as one of the members of the 7-Eleven Japan family. Crucially the 7-Eleven Japan information system is the tool to link these business connections.

There are two main columns of power in this system. One being the software and information system and the other is the hardware which supports the "7-Eleven Japan's family". Stiffness still occurs very often when the organization expands. However, 7-Eleven Japan, by using skills of "outsourcing" has prevented its internal organization from suffering from stiffness and over-growth by thoroughly utilizing external sources as if they were internal. Enjoying combined synergistic power through its business connections, its organizational strategy, skillfully taking in external sources in accordance with changes in circumstances, has produced an excellent ability to cope with changes.

Sources of Strength Hidden in the Organization Chart

The organization of 7-Eleven Japan HQ consists of major areas such as: Finance, General Affairs, Sales Administration, Recruitment, Operations, Products, Logistic Management, Facilities Construction, Accounting, Information System, Secretarial Section, Audit Section, Owner Consulting Section, and the Planning and Development Section. In the headquarters department of Product Development, a section of "information management" is set up with the purpose of collecting information on product development in the areas of "team merchandise" etc. The Development Promotion Department in the Headquarters of Logistic Development takes care of the development of original products.

Table 5-2. Organization chart of 7-Eleven Japan

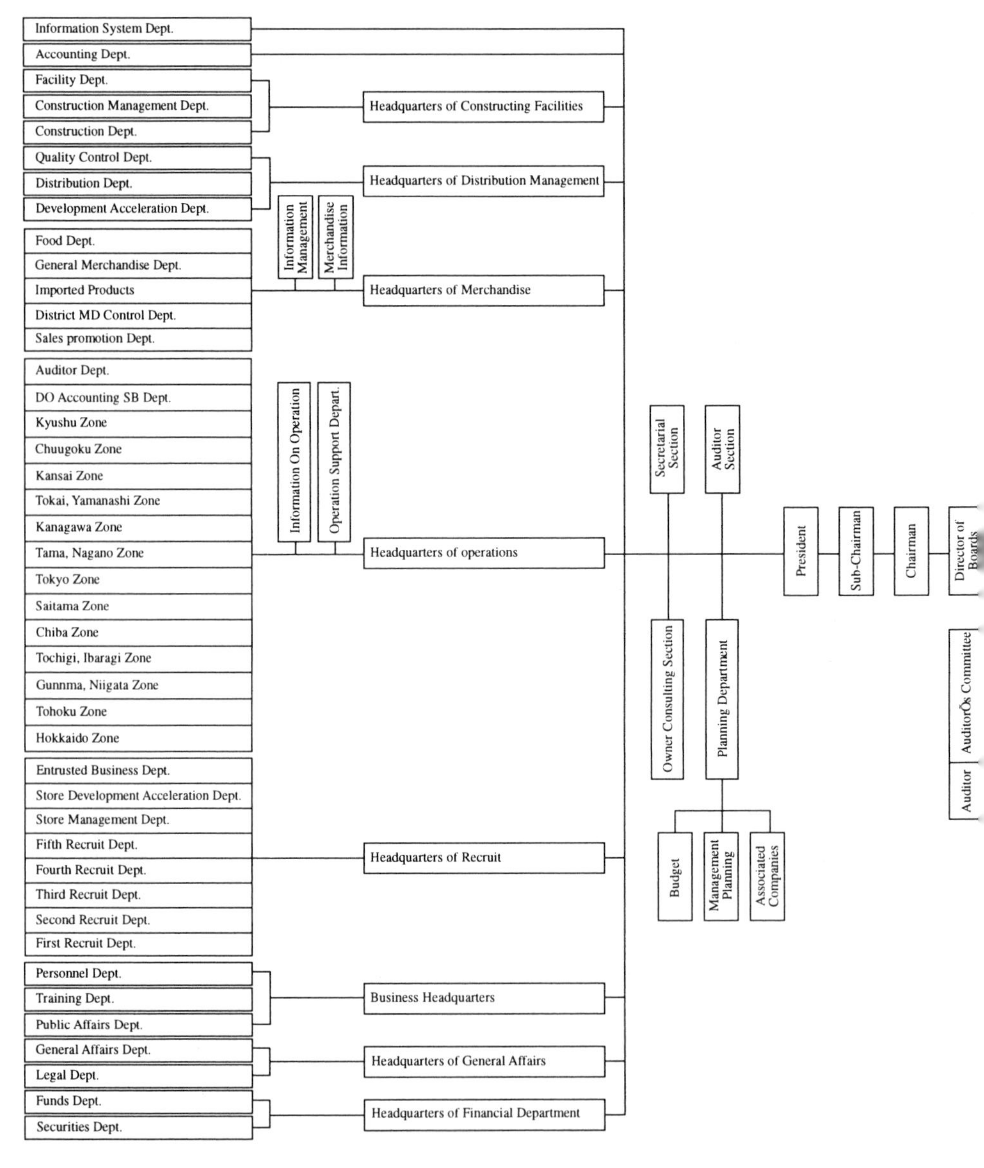

*SB stands for supervising

Source: *Periodic Securities Report '97*, page 17

Currently, customer preferences are changing more rapidly than ever and the life span of products is getting shorter. The two departments mentioned above are very important in the search for new products to "respond to changes". Of course many competitors have similar sections and people in charge, so it is not necessarily correct that only 7-Eleven Japan has this particular structure. However, within this structure of 7-Eleven Japan is perhaps where some secrets are hidden?

The strength of 7-Eleven Japan does not exist in the organizational structure itself. It could be assumed that the source of this robustness resides in its endless efforts to develop "innovative business processes" such as "consistent production, distribution and sales systems", "team merchandising" and "joint delivery". The innovation of processes creates differentiation from others and builds up its advantageous position among its competitors.

7-Eleven Japan lavishly invests in the construction of the infrastructure supporting "innovative business processes". Infrastructure both of the hardware and software type that is invisible on its organizational chart include "information systems" and "management meetings" help to connect departments organically and enhance the management efficiency of the whole organization.

Chapter 6

Any Blind Spots in 7-Eleven Japan's Strategy?

Why Are Sales of Existing Stores Growing Slowly?

As Table 6-1 shows, the decrease in 7-Eleven Japan's sales growth rate after 1992 has been a serious problem. However, from February 1997 account settlement the growth rate has returned to positive figure. The sales of game software that commenced from November 1996 amounted to 12 billion yen by March 1997. In addition, new products such as stamps and postcards have also contributed to sales growth. Since this improvement in sales is probably due to these "special procurements", it is too early to judge whether the sluggish period has come to an end.

The slow sales could be due to a number of factors such as the sluggish Japanese economy, the intensification of competition with other categories of business and competition with rival firms are other relevant issues. 7-Eleven Japan judged that the inclinations of consumers had transferred from a "price-oriented" perspective to a "value-oriented" one and thus had been deploying a strategy to offer more "value-added merchandise". This strategy brought about an immediate effect in lunch box sales that were easier to differentiate from competitors. However, consumers who have tightened their purse strings tend to go shopping either at the convenience store or to the bargain shops depending on the products they want to buy. 7-Eleven Japan still has a big task in

Table 6-1. Sales growth rate of existing stores of 7-Eleven Japan

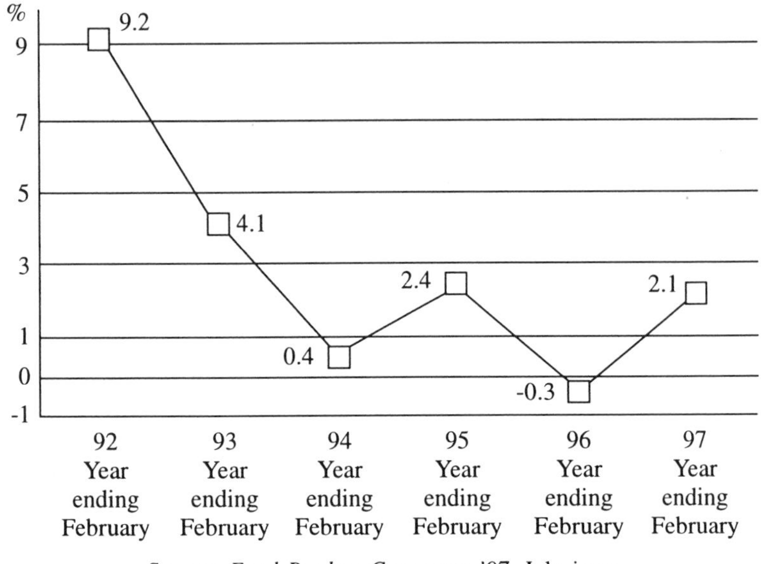

Source: *Food Product Commerce '97*, July issue

deciding how best to attract customers in times of economic slowdown.

The advantage of "offering time convenience" which convenience stores had previously used to dominate other retailer groups has begun to be eroded. Lunch boxes and other daily foodstuffs of high quality and reasonable price are selling well at food counters in department stores. This is in direct competition with the products of 7-Eleven Japan. In times of deregulation, competition with other categories of business has created new problems for 7-Eleven Japan.

Competition with rival convenience stores has also been intensifying. According to Table 2-7, the total number of convenience stores has exceeded 48,000 and this means that one store is available per population of 2,500. A coined phrase of a "Convenience Street" was created for the many areas crowded with convenience stores. Even 7-Eleven Japan cannot avoid this intensification of competition with rival firms.

Industry Structure Analysis Using the Porter Business Model

Let us look at 7-Eleven Japan from the viewpoint of the convenience industry. Using Michael Porter's analytical model of industrial structure based on the theory of industrial organization, we will clarify and comment on the structure of the convenience industry. Porter highlights five forces affecting the profit rate of an industry.

1. The threat from new entrants.
2. Hostile relationships with rival firms.
3. The threat from substitute merchandise.
4. The bargaining power of shoppers.
5. The bargaining power of manufacturers.

We will analyze the convenience industry per competitive factor.

1. Threat from new entrants

The economies of scale of the convenience industry clearly affect all purchases of materials, production, distribution, and sales. For example, chains with multiple store operations can purchase and produce in bulk quantity. The information system with its central core function of POS plays an important role in the management of products and the collection of customer's information. Therefore it could be said that the industry requires a huge initial investment in technology. It is also necessary to build up an excellent distribution system for the speedy delivery of merchandise. The building up of a large-scale distribution system together with vendors can obviously not be realized in a day. Therefore, only after years of experience can it be possible to obtain the operational know-how on the management of convenience chains. From the viewpoint of the accumulation of experience, existing chains are in an advantageous position compared to newcomers. Therefore, it could be concluded that the convenience industry is not exposed to a big threat from new entrants.

2. Hostile relationship with the existing rival chains is getting stronger

The convenience industry had been using its energy and reserves to expand and grow until the 1980s while a comparatively healthy competition had been continuing. It meant that the industry had been cultivating the market with its offer of "convenience" rather than being forced to use price competition. However, in the 1990s, the population per store became less than 3000 and the time of ruthless competition begun. Affected by a prolonged recession, the hostile relationships between rivals are becoming even stronger and this is symbolized by the competition of price reduction in the industry.

3. Threat from substitute merchandise

After the collapse of the bubble economy, the inclinations of consumers seemed to be split into two. One side represented the attitude of attaching importance to "value" rather than "price" by shopping only for quality merchandise. The other side comprised consumers looking for cheap-priced products due to the slow growth of their income. Individuals tend to purchase depending on either "value-added" merchandise or "low-priced" merchandise. Convenience chains face intensified competition with department stores in the domain of "value-added" products and with discount shops on "low-priced" merchandise. In addition, large-scale retail stores have extended their business hours and now even open on New Year's Day due to deregulation of Large-Scale Retail Stores Law. As a result of this, the advantages which the convenience industry one possessed over the other retail sectors have started to be eroded. Therefore, the pressure from substitute products is becoming much more prevalent.

4. Bargaining power of shoppers

For the convenience industry which handles mainly products related to personal effects, the differentiation of products from those of rivals is not so easy. Especially, since the collapse of the bubble economy, the purchasing patterns are becoming more diversified, symbolized by consumers' attachment to both the value/quality of merchandise and also the lower price merchandise available. Therefore, the bargaining power of shoppers with these variable options is getting stronger. However, lunch boxes, daily dishes and other such products are comparatively easier to differentiate. Each chain is trying to produce their own merchandise with the goal of getting into an advantageous position in the drive to attract shoppers.

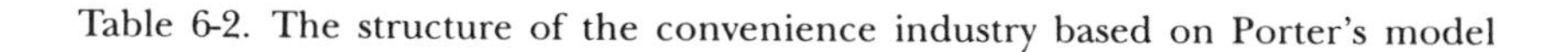

Table 6-2. The structure of the convenience industry based on Porter's model

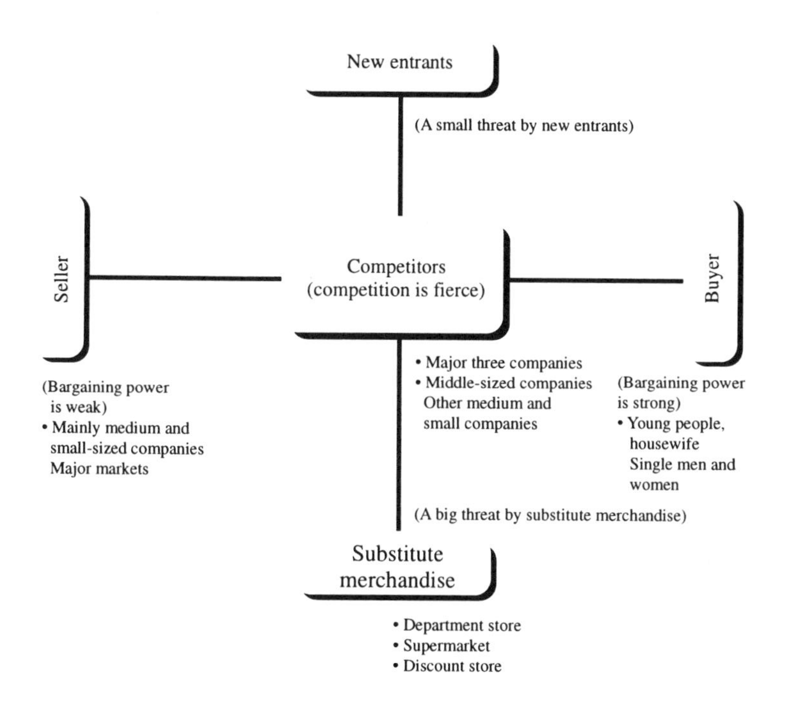

5. Bargaining power of manufacturers

The bargaining power of manufacturers in the convenience industry is weak. Conventionally, most producers of lunch boxes and daily dishes are medium- to small-sized companies with insufficient production facilities, technology, and quality control. Therefore many convenience dealers have been giving various guidance and assistance to producers in order to upgrade their abilities. In the process, the convenience industry had enhanced its dominant power over the medium- and small-sized producers.

Table 6-3. Attractiveness of the convenience industry for 7-Eleven Japan

Factor of competition	Attractiveness of the industry
Threat by new entry	+++
Hostile relations with the trade	-
Threat by substitute merchandise	--
Bargaining power of buyer	--
Bargaining power of seller	+++

In addition to medium- and small-sized producers, major manufacturers who used to have strong control over the distribution industry are losing power in their bargaining position with the convenience industry as well. This is clearly characterized by the joint development of products. Major manufacturers now develop new products based on the information on customers and the market information is provided by the convenience industry. For this reason the sales network of the convenience chains are very attractive for producers. Therefore, the convenience industry is even starting to take control of major makers by using joint development of products and its sales network.

To summarise, the attractiveness of the convenience industry for 7-Eleven Japan could be pointed out as follows:

1. 7-Eleven Japan is not highly exposed to threats from new entrants of another category of business due to its excellent information system.
2. 7-Eleven Japan has strong control over the vendors and this position in terms of bargaining makes its position in the convenience industry very strong.
3. However, competition and strong hostile relations with rival firms are intensifying year by year.
4. The threat of substitute merchandise is big and sometimes customers are attracted by large-sized retail stores and discount stores.
5. Buyers have many choices in shopping which make their bargaining power stronger.

Porter's model of the industrial structure analysis clearly shows that even 7-Eleven Japan, who possesses an overwhelming position in the convenience industry must not be over confident and complacent in its management.

Development of an Oligopoly by Three Major Companies

An oligopoly by three major companies: 7-Eleven Japan, Lawson, and Family Mart has been developing. Their shares of the total sales amount of the convenience industry have been expanding rapidly from 33% in 1992 to 45% in 1996. Currently these three major companies have been investing positively in their information systems. Consequently, they have come to take a decisive lead ahead of the other mid-size companies in the development of products.

In the metropolitan areas in particular, where competition is greatly intensifying, gaining a lead in product development can make a big difference to sales figures. The service of payment acceptance of utilities bills using the information system brings commission income and attracts many new customers. The position

Table 6-4. Oligopoly by three major companies

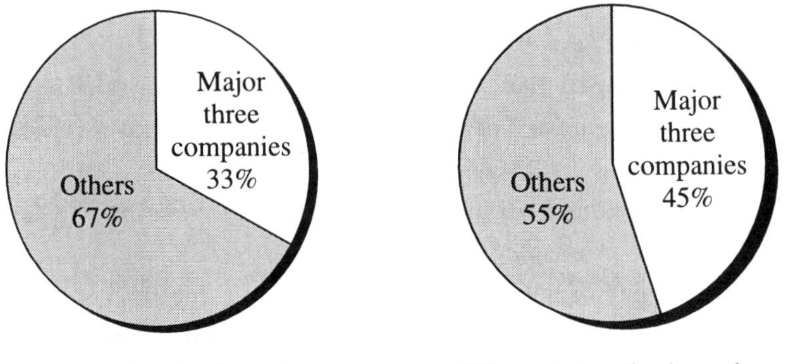

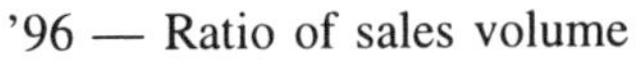

of medium- and small-sized companies who cannot invest in information systems like the major companies could soon be in an even more disadvantageous position. Information systems with rapid technology changes should be upgraded every few years and this requires a huge investment of funds. Therefore, the advantageous position of major companies will remain strong and dominant.

The shopping patterns of young people are strongly influenced by commercials, especially TV commercials. As only major company chains can allocate and afford the huge budget required for TV commercial costs, the medium and small-sized companies will further lose their competitiveness. The market share of these three major companies seems set to increase in the future.

Opposition from Existing Wholesalers Against the Establishment of an Exclusive Wholesale Operation Company

7-Eleven Japan decided from March 1998 to operate its own exclusive wholesale operation company with 18 different wholesalers handling daily merchandise. However, 7 companies out of 25 wholesalers rejected participating in this new organization and this created quite a stir. The reason for establishing this company was not only to organize more effective distribution, but also to re-organize the system to enhance the co-development of new merchandise together with manufacturers. By consolidating all transactions in this newly

Table 6-5. Wholesalers of 7-Eleven Japan and a new distribution system

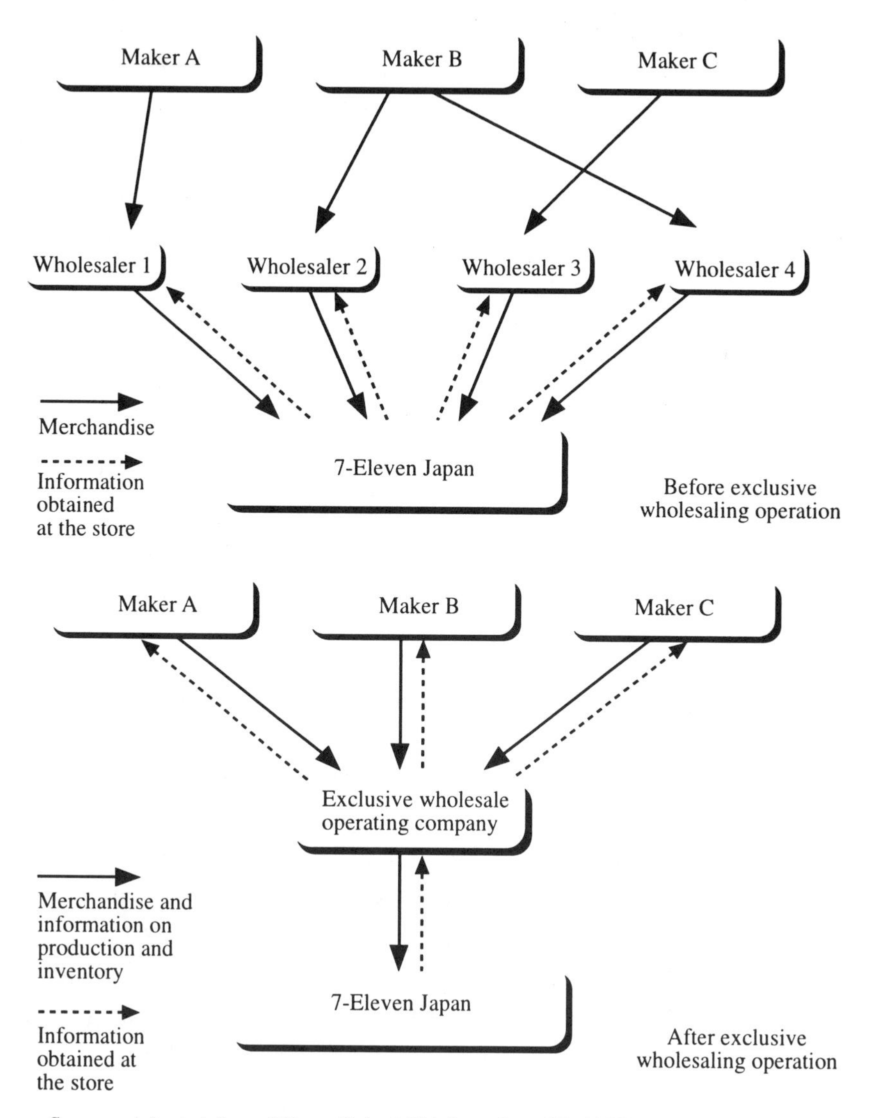

Source: Adapted from *Nihon Keizai Shinbun*, Oct. 27, 1997, morning edition

established wholesale operation, the on-line network of placement of order receipt could be simplified. In addition, manufacturers can make their products with a concrete plan as the sales information of stores is transmitted every day via this new company. Even in the co-development of new products, it is possible to achieve a more rapid development of a "hot-selling product" as any changes in customer's needs would be quickly sent to the manufacturers.

At the same time, 7-Eleven Japan would be able to obtain information on the production schedule and inventory of the manufacturers through the exclusive wholesale company. Although this system will give it benefits in the reduction of distribution costs of 2–3%, those wholesalers who did not join this new company insist that it would bring about "the loss of the conventional function of a wholesaler". Since 7-Eleven Japan with its robust sales ability requested existing wholesalers to participate in this newly established company in quite a coercive way, it encountered strong opposition from them. Manufacturers who hold influence over retailers by their domination of the wholesalers have started to keep an eye on the 7-Eleven driven distribution system. It would be problematic to see some breaks in the joint business system for 7-Eleven Japan which has a company creed of "co-existence and co-prosperity".

Opposition from Manufacturers of "Fresh Baked Bread"

7-Eleven Japan started its "fresh baked bread" business from 1994 with cooperation from the Itochu Corporation and Ajinomoto Co. Ltd. Prior to this, 7-Eleven Japan had planned to move into the bakery business jointly with Yamazaki Baking Co. Ltd., one of the major baking companies, as they had been developing a team merchandise project. However Yamazaki Baking Co. Ltd. rejected the cooperation deal with 7-Eleven Japan at the final stage. The reason for its rejection was that the independence of the manufacturer would be lost if it produces private brand products for 7-Eleven Japan. Yamazaki Baking Co. Ltd. has a very strong sales network and it was said that its pride as a major manufacturer was the reason it rejected the cooperation deal with 7-Eleven Japan. However, later on Yamazaki moved into the "fresh baked bread" business in partnership with Lawson. It is widely known that 7-Eleven Japan offers very severe contractual conditions to dealers. This shows that the way of thinking of having efficiency for efficiency's sake could not solely materialize in any joint business ventures.

Business Results of 7-Eleven Japan

From Table 6-6, using respectively the profit ratio of net worth, the profit ratio of total liabilities, it is clear that the average revenue in the last five years has increased. The sales index per person shows good stability, profitability, productivity, and growth rate at headquarters. Stability, profitability, and productivity exceed the industry average. Especially, sales per person had almost reached 100 million yen and the productivity is excellent. On the other hand, the growth rate is below that of the industry average and a cloud was hanging over the "expansion of the scale" of 7-Eleven Japan, who had already the largest number of stores in the industry.

Table 6-6. Management analysis of 7-Eleven Japan

Profit ratio of net worth		7-Eleven Japan 1997 ending February	Average in the industry, 1996
Stability	Earnings on equity	72.84%	61.37%
Profitability	Profit rate of total liabilities and net worth in use	10.69%	8.22%
Growth Potential	Five years average increase of revenue	9.35%	9.99%
Productivity	Sales per person	¥96.85 million	¥76.14 million

Source: *Nihhon Keiei shishou '97*, Autumn issue (management index of economics in Japan)

Table 6-7. Average daily sales per chain (1996, Unit Yen 10,000)

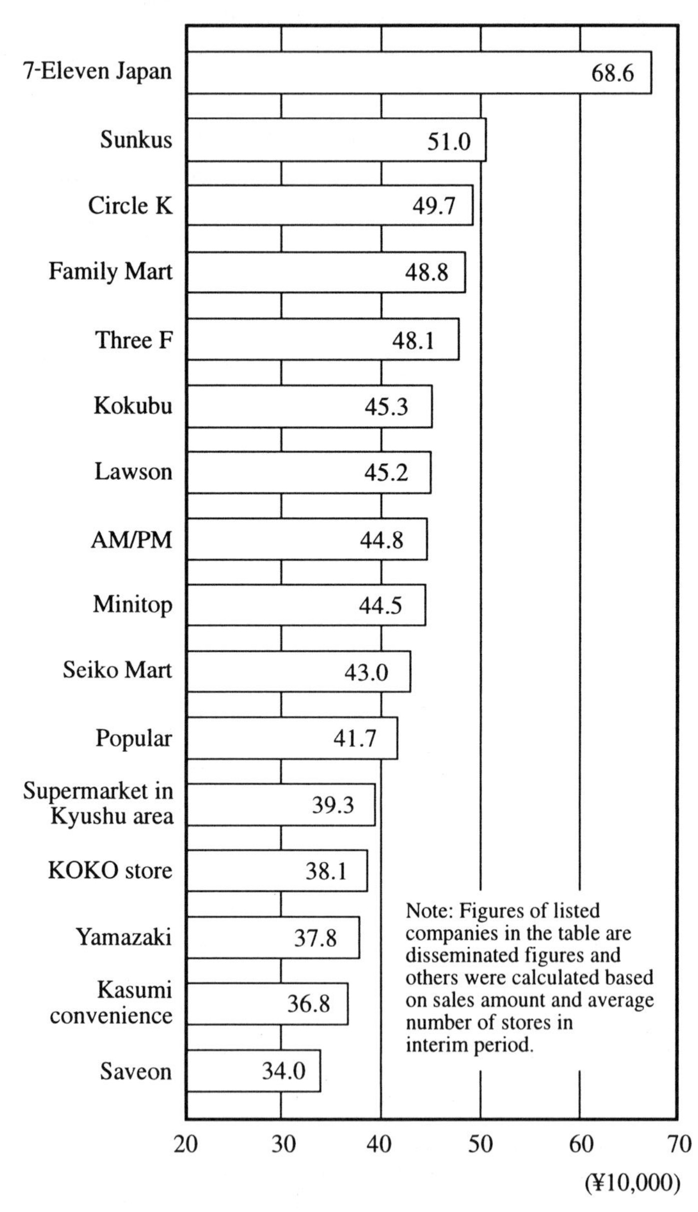

Source: *Shokuhin Shougyou (Food Commerce) '97*, July issue, page 122

As Table 6-6 shows, the average daily sales per store by far exceeds that of other convenience chains. From this fact, it is understood that 7-Eleven Japan has built up a chain store system that has relatively high gains. Management figures from headquarters and member stores clearly reflect the "robustness" of 7-Eleven Japan. However, it should not be forgotten that it is only possible to keep this "robustness" with "cooperation" from partners such as wholesalers, manufacturers, and the owner of member stores.

Vendors of Rice Products Suffer from Low Margins

7-Eleven Japan is enjoying high margins, while the vendors of rice products are suffering from low margins. It is caused by the commercialization of the vendors' sub-contractor. Theoretically, the relationship between 7-Eleven Japan headquarters and the vendor is based on equal terms, but practically the relation is more one between master and servant. How is this structure built up? The following are the causes why rice products vendors are suffering from low profitability.

Table 6-8. Business performance of 7-Eleven Japan and venders of rice product

	7-Eleven Japan	Fuji Foods Co., Ltd	Warabeya Nichiyo
Sales	¥254.6 billion	¥64.1 billion	¥63.2 billion
Ordinary profit	¥105.1 billion	¥754 million	¥850 million
Ratio of ordinary profit sales	41.2%	1.2%	1.3%
Ratio of ordinary profits of total liabilities and net worth	19.3%	2.1%	3.0%

Source: *Konbini '97*, Autumn issue, pages 126 and 127
Note: Sales of 7-Eleven Japan headquarters, but not sales of entire chain stores.

1. Due to stagnation and the intensification of competition, 7-Eleven Japan headquarters strongly requests vendors to keep up quality, while also pressurzing them to produce at lower costs. In addition, the cost of imported material has risen as the yen became weaker against the dollar.
2. The life cycle of products is getting shorter and the burden of investment in the facilities for the production of new products gets bigger. It took time for employees to get the hang of operating the new facilities and this led to inefficiencies in production and rising costs.
3. Differentiation of products develops, so the production requires a longer process and time.
4. In order to improve the profit margin, the vendor narrows down the port of suppliers. As a result of this, headquarters have a strong control over the vendors.

As Table 6-8 shows, the operating profits, ordinary profits, total liabilities and net worth of the vendor of rice products is surprisingly lower in comparison with those of 7-Eleven Japan. The convenience system that does not offer merits to the vendor will be deadlocked before long. It is a task of 7-Eleven Japan to see how it can develop "co-existence and co-prosperity" with the vendor.

Task of "Securing a Successor"

Since its establishment 7-Eleven Japan had been expanding the number of its stores by converting medium- and small-sized retail stores into its member stores. Most of them were suffering from "sluggish business performance" and the "difficulty in finding a successor to take over their business" which made them move into the new category. However, it is ironic that the current problems that owners of existing member stores face and the problems they previously experienced at the time of their conversion to convenience store do not appear to be much different.

Table 6-9. Worries of member store's owner

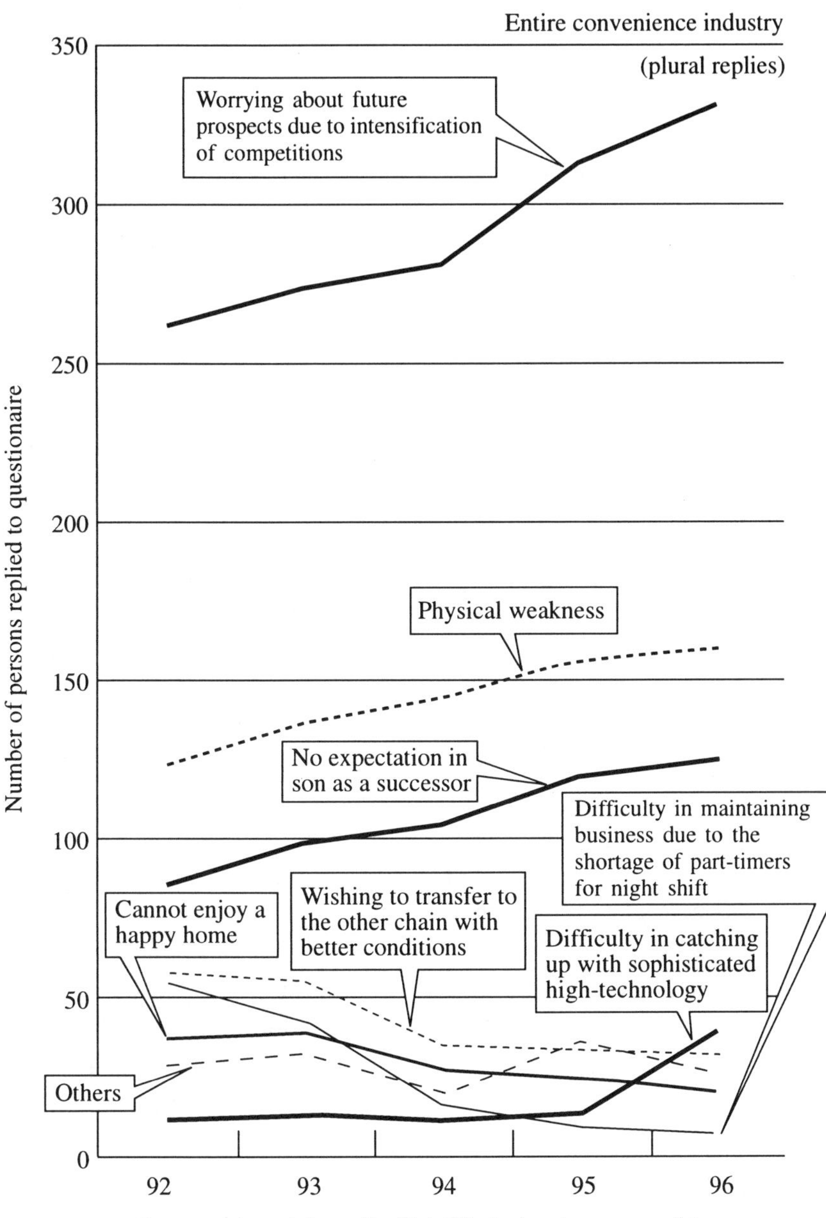

Source: Adapted from *Konbini '97*, Spring issue, page 36

Table 6-9 which shows the entire convenience store industry highlights that 7-Eleven Japan display almost the same trends. According to this, we know the problems of the owners of member stores are due to "intensification of competition", "aging of the owner", and "difficulty in finding a business successor". The problem of finding a business successor is particularly a major headache. In affluent times people look for better academic careers and generally the elite that have graduated from a first-rate university wish to get a job at a major company or a government office. Jobs as the owner of convenience stores seem unattractive not only to the elite but also to young people. It has a strong image of long working hours, monotonous work and lower income, etc. Although 7-Eleven Japan has built up a convenience chain system producing high profits, we see that it does not give enough consideration to the labor conditions of the owners of member stores. In order to secure a superior successor, 7-Eleven Japan must build up a more attractive chain system for the owners of the member stores.

Is There Any Limit to the Growth of the Convenience Industry?

At present there are approximately 48,000 convenience stores all over Japan. This figures exceeds the total number of post offices in Japan (the total number of post offices in Japan is 24,000). The number of convenience stores is catching up with the number of gas-filling stations. (There are approximately 60,000 gas stations all over Japan.) We wonder whether the existing number of convenience stores is saturated already or will the total increase further?

As Table 6-10 shows, the number of stores started to increase in the 1990s but the annual sales of the industry has grown slowly. Annual sales per store had been decreasing for five consecutive years from 1992. It clearly shows that convenience stores face problems in terms of profitability. Particularly, low levels of profitability of existing stores are quite serious concerns.

Table 6-10. Changes in the number of stores, annual income and average daily sales per store in the industry

Year	The number of stores	Growth rate	Annual sales of the industry (billion yen)	Growth rate	Average daily sales per store (thousand yen)
1982	18,800		1,812.6		275
1983	22,300	18.6	2,153.4	18.8	276
1984	25,500	14.3	2,589.7	20.3	290
1985	28,350	11.2	3,155.0	21.8	318
1986	31,150	9.9	3,789.2	20.1	348
1987	33,650	8.0	4,425.8	16.8	376
1988	35,980	6.9	5,086.0	14.9	404
1989	38,090	5.9	5,699.4	12.0	428
1990	39,614	4.0	6,280.7	10.2	453
1991	41,050	3.6	6,896.2	9.8	480
1992	42,116	2.6	6,985.9	1.3	474
1993	43,510	3.3	7,006.9	0.3	460
1994	45,207	3.9	7,126.0	1.7	456
1995	46,834	3.6	7,225.8	1.4	443
1996	48,567	3.7	7,378.0	2.1	434

Source: *Konbini '97*, Spring issue, page 27

Table 6-11 shows that the number of stores not facing competition has decreased and the number of stores facing intensified competition has increased. This clearly shows the intensification of competition with rival firms. By calculation the availability of each convenience store per population is 2,567 in Japan. It is said that stores have difficulties when the ratio of the population and the store becomes that of the magnitude 1:3000 in the US. However, we cannot easily compare with the US situation, as obviously it is a very different environment in Japan.

With further deregulation and the increasing sophistication of the information system, the possibility of expanding business by

Table 6-11. Changes in the competition of inter-convenience stores

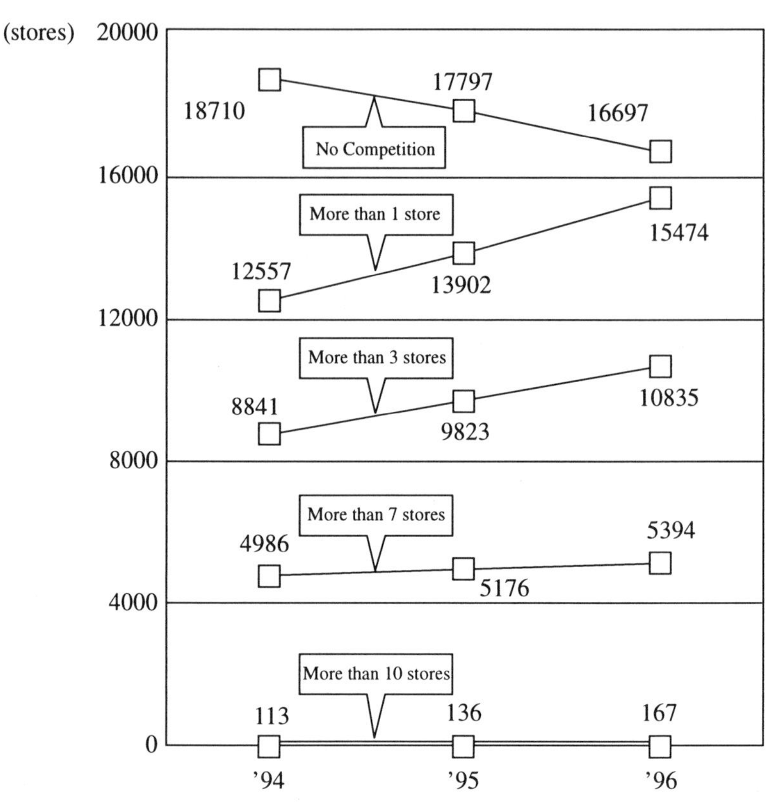

Source: *Konbini '97*, Spring issue, page 45

developing various new products and services could be more. On the other hand, we can see that the convenience industry has entered a mature stage, judging from the statistics of the decrease in the average daily sales per store, etc. Also future management will be affected by the coming era of an aging population and low birth rate as currently the main customer base for the convenience industry is centered on young people and unmarried people. With these current conflicting positive and negative factors, it will not be possible to make a precise prediction of whether stores have reached the limit and cannot absorb any more customers. Further development of the convenience industry will solely depend on whether each convenience store can make a correct response to changing times.

Is the Information System of 7-Eleven Japan Perfect?

We have repeatedly mentioned 7-Eleven Japan's "excellent ability to respond to changes". 7-Eleven Japan has rapidly grasped the changes in the preference of customers and has been successfully developing countless new products with the full use of an integrated information system. Up to now, 7-Eleven Japan has developed such innovative products as "raw vegetable cup salad", "fresh sandwiches", and "mini bowls" that has become very popular merchandises on the market. However, even 7-Eleven Japan has made several mistakes in the development of new products. For example, the mail-order business: "Shop America" started in 1990, the "mini paperback edition series" published in 1996 jointly with Shinchosha, and the "imported beer" came to abrupt halts due to unexpectedly poor sales.

7-Eleven Japan has approximately 3,000 products in each store and two-thirds of them will be replaced with new ones within a year. Thus, the life cycle of merchandise is getting shorter. However, failures like the products mentioned above was not caused by a shorter life cycle but by the wrong development ideas in misjudging customer needs. The cause of the unpopularity of "Shop America" was that customers had to bear the cost of an annual membership fee of 1,000 yen. The "mini paperback edition series" were unpopular because the literary works were completely unsuitable to the customer base of the convenience store. Imported beer was marketed without paying attention to the fact that consumers preferred domestic brand beer. Even 7-Eleven Japan with the most excellent POS system in the retail industry could make mistakes. Since 1997, 7-Eleven Japan has been using the fifth integrated information system with further upgraded functions, responding to the changing circumstances. There may be no end to the amount of upgrades to the information system.

Environmental Problems Surrounding the Convenience Store Industry

Japan had pledged, along with other participating countries at the Kyoto Environmental conference, to make an effort to reduce the level of greenhouse gases to 6% in an effort to combat the problems of global warming. It is quite natural that people concerned with environmental issues could worry about the convenience industry, as it operates 24 hours and requires high frequency deliveries. 7-Eleven Japan was, of course, included in the strong criticism because high frequency delivery were said to cause traffic jams and increase exhaust gas pollution.

7-Eleven Japan counterargued against these criticisms as follow:

1. When 7-Eleven Japan established business in 1974, the numbers of deliveries had reached 70 vans per day per store but they have successfully reduced this number to 9 vans per day per store through the efforts of rationalization of the "joint delivery system".
2. 7-Eleven Japan considers that its efficient distribution system contributes to the easing of traffic jams.

However, it is easy to understand why high frequency delivery represented by the three times per day delivery of lunch boxes can provoke some debate. Even the 24-hour operation mode is criticized by many quarters in light of environmental problems, and even social problems like the increase of crime. 7-Eleven Japan has decided to invest 5 billion yen on electricity-saving equipment to be installed at all of its chain stores by February 1998. This equipment is designed to save the electricity of electric lights in and outside the stores and also the electricity of air-conditioners simultaneously.

It would cut down more than 13% of the carbon dioxide emissions in comparison with the emission level from the 1990s.

We can understand 7-Eleven Japan's quick responses to various critics, but the concept of time convenience will collapse if it stops its 24-hour operation and the solution of problems will remain obscure in the future. The protection of the global environment is an unavoidable theme for many companies. Even the existence of the convenience industry itself could be endangered if 7-Eleven Japan, who is the leader in the industry, cannot propose appropriate measures to ease these many environmental concerns.

Chapter 7

The Fifth Integrated Information System Connecting Chain Stores Utilizing Satellite Communications

The General Concept of the Fifth Integrated Information System

7-Eleven Japan introduced the fifth integrated information system in November 1997. This system was jointly developed by 12 companies such as Nomura Research Institute (NRI), NEC, Microsoft and others in order to network 50,300 terminals of the headquarters, member stores, regional offices and customers, which comprise the following components.

1. Store system
2. System for order placement, distribution and customer request
3. Network system
4. Groupware system
5. Transmission system of multimedia information
6. POS information system
7. POS store register system

All of these systems were operative by the summer of 1999. Total investment costs will amount to 60 billion yen and it will be the largest network of the distribution industry in the world. The biggest feature of this system is the introduction of satellite communications. Information from headquarters to stores and regional offices is transmitted by satellite links and information

Table 7-1. Fifth integrated information system

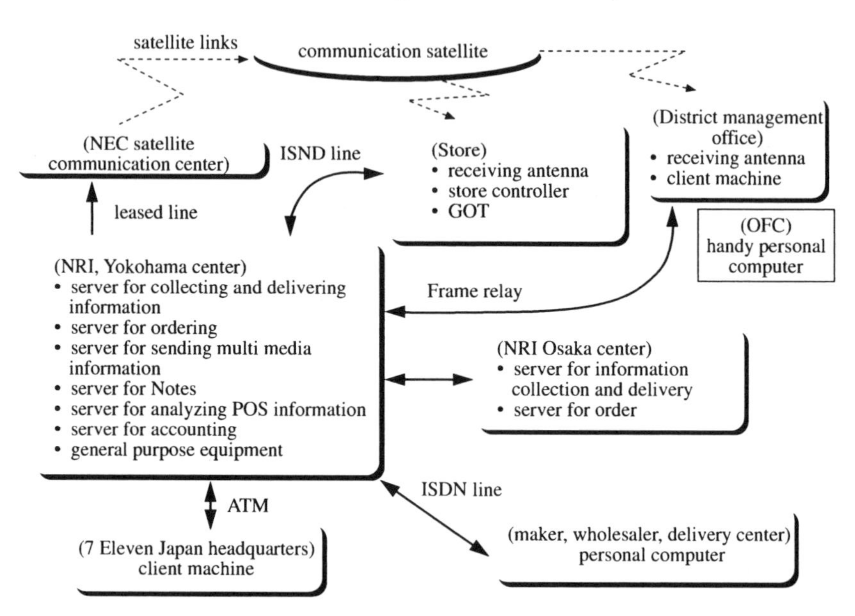

Source: *Nikkei Information Strategy '98*, January issue, the above diagram was simplified based on the contents of page 9.

from stores to regional offices is transmitted by ISDN links. These transmission speeds are 45 times quicker in comparison with the previous speed and consequently, communication costs will be reduced by approximately 20%. An antenna for the game software demonstration machine produced by Dig Cube Corp. is set up in the store and is also used as a reception antenna as well. Information received from the headquarters is indicated on the display of the store controller or GOT.

Order information from the store and POS information are sent to Nomura Souken, Yokohama Center via ISDN links. The server for orders and the server for collecting and distribution information will also be set up at the Osaka center to prepare for troubles and disasters. Portable personal computers are available for operation field counselor (OFC), this enables the regional offices and stores to be able to access information directly from the headquarters.

Due to the increase in the number of new stores, the business performance of the headquarters of 7-Eleven Japan has been improving. However, the sales performances of existing stores have been growing slowly. The biggest reason for introducing this new system is to provide an effective guidance system to stores. To fulfill this purpose, the transmission of multimedia information such as characters, still pictures, animations and sound, in order to create "the store with highly sellable merchandise and services" plays a very important role. In addition, it is a system which is able to respond to changing times such as deregulation and electronic money.

Utilizing "Animations", "Still Pictures" and "Sound" for the Construction of an Attractive Store with Heavy-selling Items and Services

TV commercials can have a big impact on the sale of merchandise. Until the new technological development brought about by the 5th information system, customers could not see commercials broadcast in the store. The new system was provided with a function to enable the display of TV commercials with sound. At the same time 7-Eleven Japan urged chain stores to sell on a priority basis the specific products that receive strong support from the TV commercials. 7-Eleven Japan has received much favorable attention as a pioneer of this new skill of "sales closely tied to TV commercials".

The new information system can also furnish chain stores with on-screen images of a successful product display. Therefore, it is possible to see tests pictures of how products should be best displayed in the store. Previously, it was very difficult to communicate accurately what was the most attractive manner of display by explaining in words only. Thus, it has become easier to make more possible the ideal concept of "the attractive store with heavy-selling items and services".

Sales of merchandise are strongly influenced by the weather. Therefore, the new information system is also provided with a function for providing visual weather information displays. In addition, not only the weather information of the surrounding area is included but also the weather information covering wider areas. Due to this, 7-Eleven Japan has often succeeded in attracting people who are planning to go to holiday resorts as they access the system to check the weather.

Using This New System for Smooth Communication with Employees

The new system is also helpful as a communication tool between the store manager and employees. As the convenience store opens 24 hours, it very often happens that workers and managers do not meet each other due to different shift times. In order to avoid this communication gap, a voice-input system is incorporated in the new system, so that all employees who come to the store can hear the store manager's instruction by voice input. As part-time workers with less experience can also hear the store manager's instruction by voice, it will be helpful for making order placements more accurate. Input of handwritten letters and illustrations are also allowed, so that communication using both eyes and ears becomes possible using this system.

This new system can be used as a tool for communications from employees to the store manager, from the OFC to the store manager and from employee to employee. In general, information sharing is thus made more effective and efficient in terms of store management. The fifth integrated information systems represents 7-Eleven Japan's strong will to construct "an attractive store with heavy-selling goods and services".

Utilization of Multimedia Information for Sales Promotion

At every chain store of 7-Eleven Japan, approximately 70% of the merchandise will be replaced with new ones within a year. Since the preference of customers changes rapidly, the life cycle of merchandise is getting shorter year by year. Therefore, new products come on the shelf one after another and poor-selling items are quickly removed. Until the new information system was introduced, 7-Eleven Japan had distributed information on material of new merchandise in the form of printed matter to each member store. However, it takes a long time and means substantial costs to prepare and distribute the materials of new products that total over 2,000 items a year. There are also many unsuccessful products that are removed from the shelf after only two weeks. Therefore, 7-Eleven Japan cannot expect this to be an effective way of sales promotion when it requires a week to prepare and distribute the material. The fifth integrated information system enables the online transmission of material as image information to the store all at once. It shortens the lead-time drastically and cuts down the cost of paper and distribution. The system with this function of sending multimedia information such as images will be indispensable for sales promotion during "times of change".

An Elaborate Marketing Plan Using a "Data Warehouse"

The "POS information system" component of the fifth integrated information system is attracting much attention and was operative from spring 1998. A new POS information system called "data warehouse" has the capability to accumulate information of item-by-item management for about 400 days in the 6 terabyte capacity of its parallel-processing supercomputer.

Before this system was developed, the conventional system was designed to grasp "what, how, when, and to whom merchandise was sold". Now this new system can analyze "what type of products are sold together". This method to further grasp the customer's shopping trends is called a "basket analysis" in the sense that the store can grasp the content of a customer's shopping basket. By utilizing this basket analysis, it is possible to develop an elaborate marketing plan.

Further developments include "data-mining technology" to search specific and necessary information from the huge mountain of information, and "push technology" which are used to update automatically information from headquarters. 7-Eleven Japan aims at making order placement more accurate by further substantiation of POS information.

Chapter 8

The Convenience Store Industry Changing with the Times

Stamps and Rice Are Now on Sale at the Convenience Store

Due to deregulation in 1996, it became possible to sell stamps, postcards, revenue stamps, rice and other new products at the convenience store. More than 80% of all convenience chain stores now handle the sale of stamps, postcards, and revenue stamps and this area of sales amounts to some 100 billion yen per year. Not only does this service contribute to the increase in sales figures, but it also attracts many customers resulting in incidental shopping as well. More than 90% of all convenience stores now sell rice and this contributes in particular to capturing the housewife bracket as a new customer type. This customer group had previously seldom shopped in the convenience store. Each convenience store comes up with methods such as assisting the farm in producing better quality products and improving the distribution system. Offering goods related closely to daily life enables a store to expand the base of its customers. We are likely to see changes in the selection of goods in the coming years in Japan due to an aging population with a low birth rate.

Table 8-1. Deregulation area concerning convenience industry

- Sales of stamps, postcards, revenue stamps
- Sales of rice
- Sales of travelling tickets, tours
- Liquor license
- Sales of medical supplies

- Handling foreign exchange
- Self-service operation at the gas-filling station
- In-store installment of bank ATM

Note: Regulation of sales of stamps, rice and travelling tickets has already been eased. As for others, it is expected to take place in the near future.

High Expectations for Deregulation of Medical Supplies

In expectation of deregulation in the sales of medical supplies in 1998, each convenience store is preparing its entry to this field. Which medical supplies can be handled safely by convenience stores is currently under study by the Ministry of Health and Welfare. General estimates about the size of this market are well over 100 billion yen.

In order to cope with the times when consumers have strong concerns about health and fitness, each convenience store is strongly enthusiastic. However, handling medical supplies will pose many problems. Therefore, the range of medical supplies handled by convenience stores will be rather limited from the viewpoint of safety even if deregulation is enforced. Sales of medicine with strong side affects will be prohibited. One of the goods highly anticipated and most marketable at the store are nutrient tonics.

There is much opposition from the existing pharmacies and drugstores about the entry of convenience industry because they want to defend their sales right of heavy-selling products such as cold medicine, anodyne, and stomach medicine. It is apparent that the medicine industry will give various reasons for their opposition and bring pressure to bear on the government. Besides the above-

Table 8-2. Changes in the number of stores handling liquor and sales of liquor

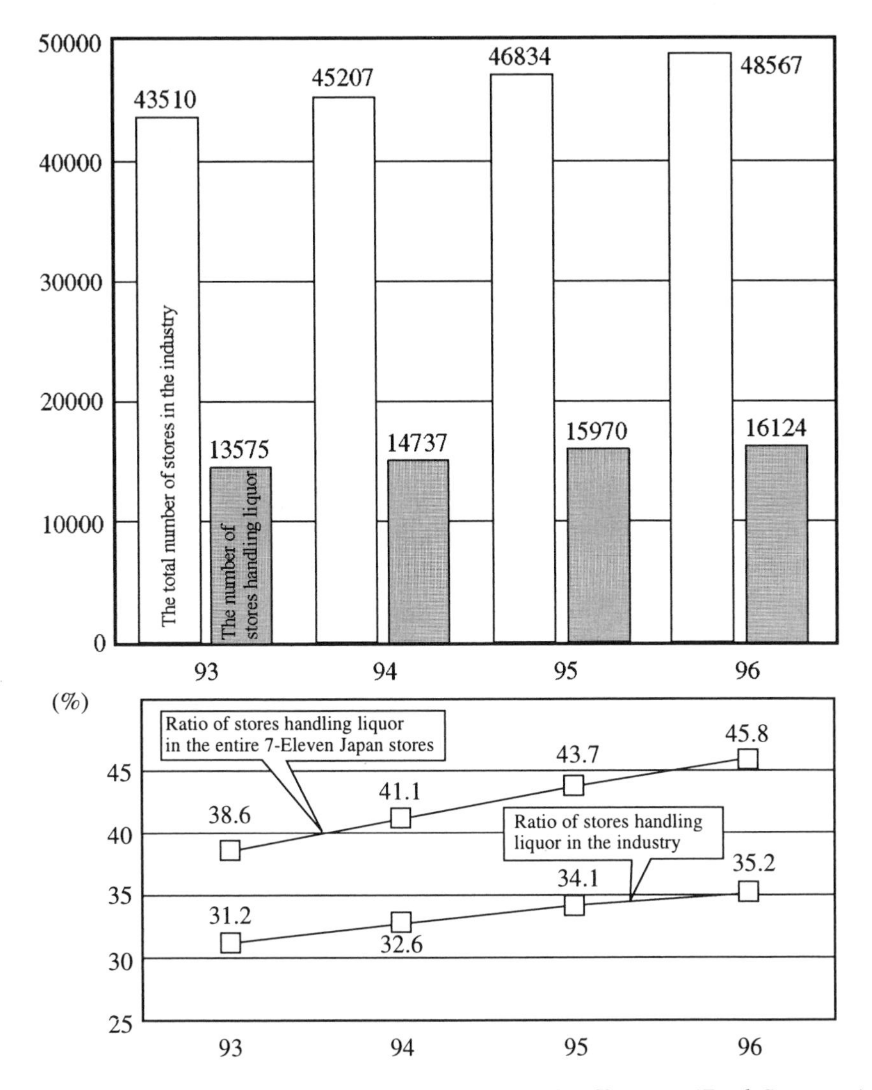

Source: *Konbini '97*, Spring issue, page 30 and *Shokuhin Shougyou (Food Commerce)* '97, July issue, page 124.

mentioned problems, there are many foreseeable stumbling blocks as to whether pharmaceutical companies and wholesale stores with long-term close relationships with the pharmacies and drugstores will be able to establish a system capable of satisfying the demands of the convenience stores. However, the sale of medical supplies at convenience stores which are opened 24 hours and 365 days will provide great benefits to consumers. There is great potential for medical supplies to be the main selling product of the convenience stores in the future.

Making an All-Out Effort to Obtain a Liquor License

Deregulation of the liquor license is under study now. 35% of convenience stores in Japan sell liquor and the sales figures of liquor account for some 20% of the total sales of stores. This means a 20% difference in the total sales of stores, depending on the availability of liquor or not. Therefore, it is quite natural that each convenience chain tries to increase the ratio of liquor selling stores.

If special measures for the protection of liquor stores were abolished, it would pave the way for 7-Eleven Japan to obtain liquor licenses together with those already obtained by occupation change of liquor store. One of the main factors in the big jump of the sales

Table 8-3. Ratio of sales of liquor in the industry

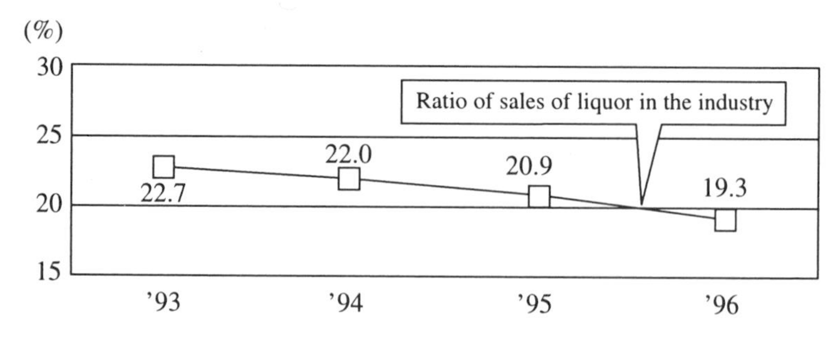

Note: Ratio of sales of liquor in the industry means the ratio of sales of liquor accounting for total sales of stores handling liquor.

Source: *Konbini '97*, Spring issue, page 30 and *Shokuhin Shogyo (Food Commerce) '97*, July issue, page 124.

figures of 7-Eleven Japan is due to the high ratio of stores handling sales of liquor. That is why an average daily sales of 7-Eleven Japan considerably exceeded the average daily sales of the industry.

In order to grow from younger customer bases, this liquor license is what convenience stores want to obtain. Competitions to get this liquor license will be intensified furthermore from now on.

New Trends in the Relationship between Gas-filling Stations and Convenience Stores

There are turbulent developments in the gas-filling station industry these days with stiff-price competition and the closing down of many stations. In 1998, the lifting of a ban on self-service in gas filling was expected to take place. What sort of opportunities can the convenience industry receive with this new style of self-service and by the closing down of many stations? The relationship between the convenience industry and gas-filling stations can be highlighted in two key aspects: a) re-use of the ex-site of the gas-filling stations, and b) convenience stores that are built next to gas-filling stations.

In 1996, more than 1500 gas-filling stations were closed down and these trends were expected to increase after 1997. Parking availability is a critical concern for convenience stores located along a road. This is the main reason why ex-sites of gas-filling stations of large areas of nearly 300 tsubo on average (one tsubo is approximately 3.3 m^3) could be a target of the convenience stores. Customers who came to the convenience store by car tend to "buy more at one time" so the average purchase amount is quite high. As a result, convenience stores could achieve great sales if they can attract more customers with cars. Regarding convenience stores combined with gas-filling stations, petroleum distributors have already begun to develop some smaller scale convenience stores. It has been 10 years since the Fire Service Law was eased in 1987, but these small stores can hardly be expected to be successful.

The main reason is that the synergy in these kinds of stores will not be easily generated as both sides of the business need a lot of help respectively. However, since 1998 after self-service gas filling was permitted, the situation started to change. As the number of personnel responsible for the filling service will be reduced, they can be transferred to work in the convenience stores. If the gasoline volume could be indicated on the screen of the register at the counter, customers would be able to pay for the gasoline at the counter of the convenience store. Thus, a synergy effect in terms of costs is expected. On the other hand, problems also exist. It was pointed out that Japanese customers are somewhat reluctant to do their shopping for food and gasoline in the same place. In addition, there are many managers at the gas-filling stations who do not want to use their workers in the convenience stores. Some 30% of the total profits of gas-filling stations are derived from the sales of car accessories other than gasoline. These profitable services include mechanical work and performing safety checks for cars.

The possible development of new stores at gas-filling stations by convenience stores solely depends on their efforts to sufficiently persuade customers on the merits of shopping at combined stores. They must also make the owners of the gas stations understand the possible merits of the synergy and the expertise that convenience stores can bring.

Itochu Corp. Became the Largest Shareholder in Family Mart

In March 1998, Seiyu Ltd. decided to sell all of its shares in Family Mart to the Itochu Corp. This purchase, together with its previously held share in Family Mart, meant that the Itochu Corp.'s share holding ratio of Family Mart rose to 30.6%, thus it became the majority shareholder. Itochu Corp. has appointed the next president of Family Mart, but this is a first full-scale move for Itochu Corp. into the retail business. Itochu Corp. had previously limited its business activities to wholesale and distribution areas and it will have to learn to deal with downstream business and upstream business in a consistent way.

On the other hand, Seiyu Ltd was said to sell its shares in Family Mart, in order to obtain depreciation funds to settle bad loans caused by the Saison Group. Seiyu Ltd said that it will now focus its resources on its core business of supermarkets. However, the question remains why did it sell Family Mart, which was a blue-chip company and is in the same line of business?

The relationship between Itochu Corp. and Ito-Yokado Group has been intimate since the founding of 7-Eleven Japan. The Itochu Corp. served to bridge the gap between 7-Eleven Japan and Southland USA and acted as an intermediary in the opening of 7-Eleven Japan shops in the Chinese market. Furthermore, the Itochu Corp has various business tie-ups with 7-Eleven Japan in the domestic market in different kinds of business, most prominently of course the "business of fresh baked bread" which has become very popular.

Needless to say, 7-Eleven Japan and Family Mart have a sharp rival relationship in business and we wonder what will become of the Itochu Corp.'s relationship with both 7-Eleven Japan and Family Mart? 7-Eleven Japan is now worried that its know-how will leak to its rival. Therefore, it could be probable that 7-Eleven Japan will downsize its business transactions with Itochu Corp. However, as Itochu Corp. and 7-Eleven Japan have developed many joint enterprises, the risk will be very big if they completely and abruptly terminate their relationship.

It would be possible to take the view that Itochu Corp. could set up individual subsidiaries to deal with both Family Mart and 7-Eleven Japan separately. This would seek to avoid the leak of each company's know-how and thus try to maintain its relationship on a stable basis. Another view is the possibility of the unification of the information and distribution system of both companies.

To take an extreme view, this could even mean the acquisition of Family Mart by 7-Eleven Japan. However, at this point, things are very much in the speculative stage but it is quite certain that the takeover of Family Mart by Itochu Corp. will greatly affect the structure of the convenience industry in general.

Expanding Serviceability by Introducing Home-Delivery Operations

Several convenience stores have moved to provide different types of home-delivery service. They aim to expand their customer base with this additional service which greatly reduces customer's effort in "going to the shop and bringing home products". For example, AM-PM accepts telephone orders of merchandise and has started a home-delivery service by charging 2000 Yen per parcel at a time. Mainline merchandise such as paper diapers for old people, baby items and even products exclusively made for home-delivery are prepared. The AM-PM strategy is to attract those who are handicapped and who are not able to regularly visit the store as a new customer group.

It is expected that the demand for this sort of service will be more in light of the increase in the aging population and it would be highly probable that "services unifying sales and delivery" will be further expanded.

For example, Sunkist has started her own home-delivery service in order to deliver merchandise that the customer orders by multimedia station (MMS). This delivery service using MMS is steadily increasing and customers can enjoy simultaneously the two different services of "one-stop shopping" and the "free from carrying products home task".

The main advantage of the convenience store is that it possesses the flexibility to keep up with changes in the social structure in a rapid way and through the progress of information equipment is able to develop new services one after another.

New Entrants from Different Categories of Business

New entrants to the convenience industry from different categories of business has been expanding. In particular, convenience stores run by various railway companies have started to operate very widely. The following companies have opened convenience stores.

1. East Japan Railway	"JC"
2. West Japan Railway	"Heart IN"
3. Hanshin Electric Railway Co., Ltd./ Keihan Electric Railway Co., Ltd./ Nankai Electric Railway Co., Ltd.	"Anthree"
4. Odakyu Electric Railway	"Odakyu OX"

Railway-oriented convenience stores are characterized by their good locations. They are usually set up in the station and surrounding area with obvious geographical advantages for catching customer traffic.

With regard to the Shosha (General Trading Company), Itochu Corp. obtained majority shares in Family Mart. This convenience store will receive strong management from a general trading company. This is the first of its kind and will be watched with keen interest.

Sumitomo Corporation has established a drive-through convenience chain store. This type of store could be seen as a new type of store compatible with the motoring age.

"Business convenience" which provide business related services, i.e. copying, documentation, printing, binding, business machines rental and rental space are already in the market. These stores do not quite belong to the conventional sector of the convenience industry as convenience chains so far have been mainly targetted at the individual customer. It is possible that with higher degree of outsourcing used by companies, "business convenience" could be established as a new category of business for convenience stores.

Chapter 9

Progress in the Unification of the Retail and Banking Sectors

Unifying Cashing and Shopping

Currently, some of the convenience chains provide in-house cash dispensers (CD) for credit cards. Credit card holders can enjoy cashing services with Lawson's in-house CD not only with the credit card issued by the Daiei Group but also with several other credit card companies.

In-house CDs installed in the convenience stores are expected to pull in more customers, most obviously credit card holders. These customers predictably stay to buy something after they have just made a withdrawal by CD. Thus, cashing and shopping could be combined which is profitable for stores and useful for customers. However, CD machines take up space in the store and probably this function will be integrated with the multifunctional terminal, i.e., MMS in the future.

Credit card payments exclude MMS products because Lawson accepts only cash payment at the counter for most MMS products. The reason is: Lawson considers communications with customers at the register very important. The installation of CD machines for credit cards could be seen as a first step toward "unifying retail and banking roles".

Banking Industry and Convenience Store Cooperation with ATM Installations?

The banking industry has been expanding their retail bases by opening unmanned ATM-only branches. Furthermore, there are other banking sectors expecting future deregulation, which are in the process of studying the possibilities of installing ATMs in convenience stores. For customers of convenience stores, it would be a further convenience to be able to make a withdrawal from an ATM which is opened 24 hours and 365 days. Convenience stores can also expect more customers in addition to credit card holders. Thus, the introduction of ATMs would seem to be able to attract many new customers.

On the other hand, key issues include the management of this 24-hour service by the banking industry and the security factor in the convenience stores. Circle K. Japan has been installing ATMs of Tokai Bank, Ltd. since July 1997 in some of its stores. Some 200 customers per day on average make cash withdrawals from the ATMs and 20% out of the 200 customers are found to do some "incidental shopping" after withdrawing cash. So the unification of the retail with banking industries is already well underway.

Buying and Selling Dollars at the Convenience Store?

With the revised Foreign Exchange and Foreign Trade Control Law enforced from April 1998, foreign currency exchange will be completely liberalized. This means the time will come when anybody can exchange foreign currency due to this Big Bang financial deregulation. Some companies in the convenience industry are already studying the possibilities of moving into this sector.

Glory, Ltd., a maker of money handling machines has developed an automatic exchange equipment specialized in foreign currency. It plans to sell this equipment to convenience stores and others.

However, it is not so easy to predict how many people will use this equipment in the convenience stores.

Apart from stores located in business areas and the surrounding areas of airports and hotels, the market scale for the entire convenience industry all over Japan is not big enough to be profitable. Furthermore, stores must bear the risk of floating exchange rates and the problems of security management exist. It would seem to be a rather limited service for the time being.

Unification of Retail and Banking Sectors in England

In England, the major retail industry moves into the banking sector and "unification of retail and banking sector" have been proceeding rapidly. There are many things which the Japanese convenience industry can learn from the unification of retail and banking sectors in England. There is good reference data available for studying the prospective future moves of the convenience industry.

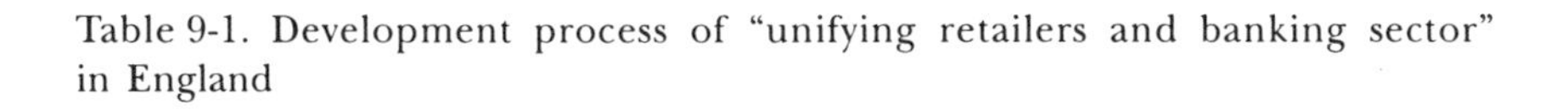

Table 9-1. Development process of "unifying retailers and banking sector" in England

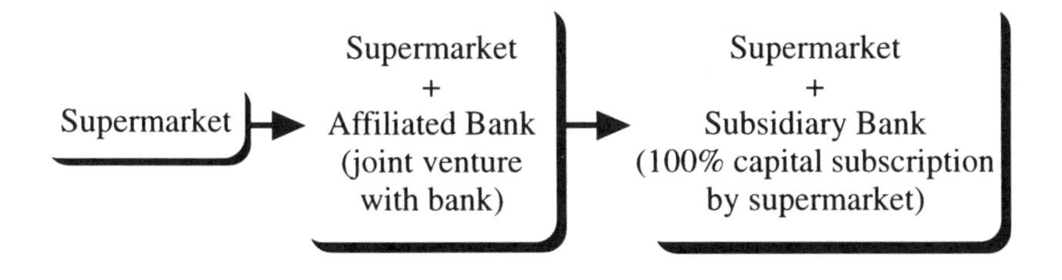

In 1997, the major supermarket chain, Sainsbury, established the Sainsbury Bank jointly with the Bank of Scotland. As the supermarket chain took over the leadership of the bank, it could be called a "supermarket bank". Sainsbury also entered a partnership with Abbey National, a financial institution based in England in the same year. The Sainsbury Bank focuses on the areas of saving deposits, non-collateral loans, property financing, and the payment of credit cards, etc. It contracts out an ATM network and accounting system to the associate bank to achieve lower operating costs.

Sainsbury supermarkets prepare leaflets of the bank in the store and provides a special corner where customers can make a direct call to the telephone center of the bank. Customers therefore can open a bank account, apply for loans or make balance inquiries by phone using this direct line or by calling from home.

In the retail industry in England, an oligopoly of six major supermarkets has been developing which account for some 70% of the total market. The supermarket is an indispensable part of people's life. It is the strategy of the supermarket to use all its know-how accumulated so far in order to attract customers to the banking sector. Since supermarket banks offer customers higher interest rates than those of existing banks, Sainsbury Bank has already obtained accounts of 400,000 people. It will not be difficult for further development of financial instruments and sales. It is quite probable that supermarkets, because of their increased confidence, will not opt for a joint venture subsidiary with a bank but for a single subsidiary 100% owned by the supermarket.

Actually Marks and Spencer Financial Services, 100% owned by the department store and established in 1985, has grown to be such a successful enterprise that it has become the leading profit contributor of the entire group. The success of supermarket banking in England indicates that "unification of retail and banking sector" will progress further in future.

Unification of Retail and Banking Sectors Progresses in Japan

With Japan's Big Bang in April 1998, the retail industry has also started to prepare their move into the banking sector. Credit Saison which belongs to the Saison Group, has already obtained 15 million customers' credit membership and accumulated huge amount of customer data. It has introduced a parallel-processing supercomputer to study the methods of using their customer base information for marketing purposes. Furthermore, the Saison Group owns Saison Securities Co., Saison Life Insurance Co., Ltd., and All State Automobile and Fire Insurance Co., Ltd. Thus it has already made its strategic movement to the area of securities and life insurance.

Table 9-2. Capital contributions by associated companies in Saison Group

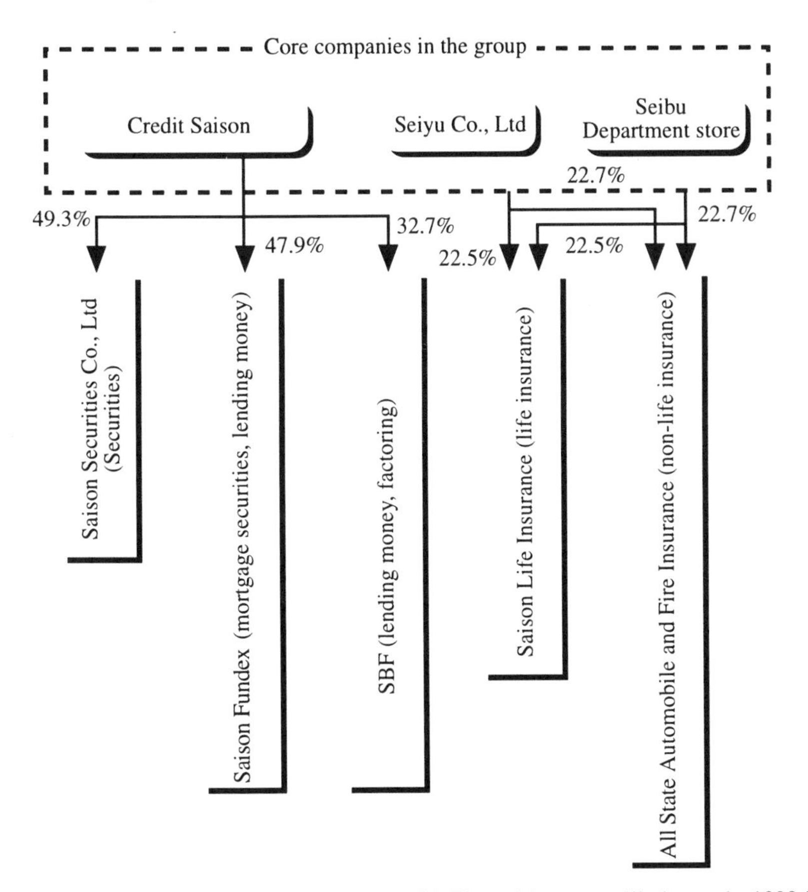

Source: *1998 Kinyuu ha Kou Kawaru*, page 56. Financial sector will change in 1998 in this way.

Credit Saison Co., Ltd also has a plan to tie up with American Express International which has many card members from the advanced age group and is aiming at the expansion of its customer base of credit-card holders.

A big focus of the Big Bang is how to incorporate private financial assets amounting to 1200 trillion yen. The Saison Group, holding many retail businesses with close contact to customers on a daily basis, will probably have the advantage over others "when retail and banking sector will be united". Jusco Group has AEON Credit Service with over 5 million members. Together with the number of its supermarkets, and Minitop a convenience store, its entire number of stores exceeds 1,000. So it will have a strong foundation for developing financial business.

Jusco Group is said to be considering the establishment of an affiliated bank like the "Supermarket bank" in England. Also it is planning to introduce a network system to deal with the sale of bonds and other financial business for customers at home and abroad, and develops a financial "unification of retail and banking sector".

The Daiei Group has Daiei OMC, a credit company and cardholders can use any CD machine in the Lawson chain. The Daiei group is very positive in acquiring know-how in the area of financial services and has participated very often in the practical experiment of electronic money "visa cash" that has been held in Kyoto since October 1997.

7-Eleven Japan, on the contrary, is not taking much action at present, but has started the introduction of the fifth integrated information system that has a function to connect with banking facilities.

After the Japanese Big Bang, the information concerning customers and retail stores will be even more a precious "management resource" than ever. Methods on how to utilize this precious management resource will be the key point to establish an advantageous position in competition.

Electronic Money and the Convenience Industry

Currently, the commercial possibilities of electronic money have been tried in many countries. If electronic money materialize, the advantages which the convenience industry would receive would be enormous as it will no longer be necessary to use cash in the store. Although there is no clear definition of electronic money, it is generally understood as "digitized currency". Two definitions of electronic money exist:

1. "IC card type electronic money" works like a credit card.
2. "Network type electronic money" conducts payment on a network.

It is assumed that "IC card type electronic money" will establish closer connections with the convenience industry in the near future.

Table 9-3. History of currency in practical use, changing together with the times

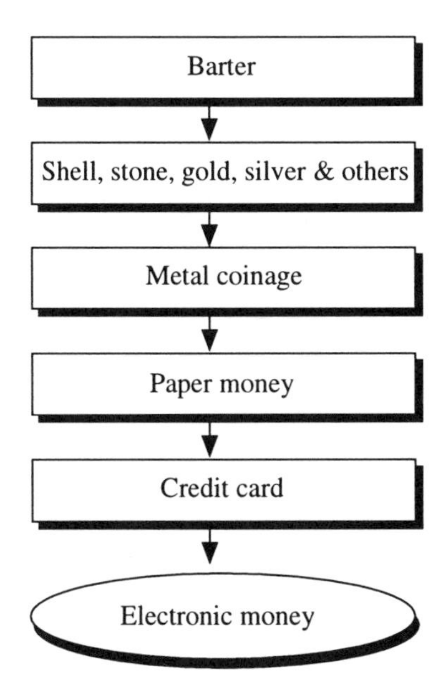

Table 9-4. Example of IC type electronic money in practical use

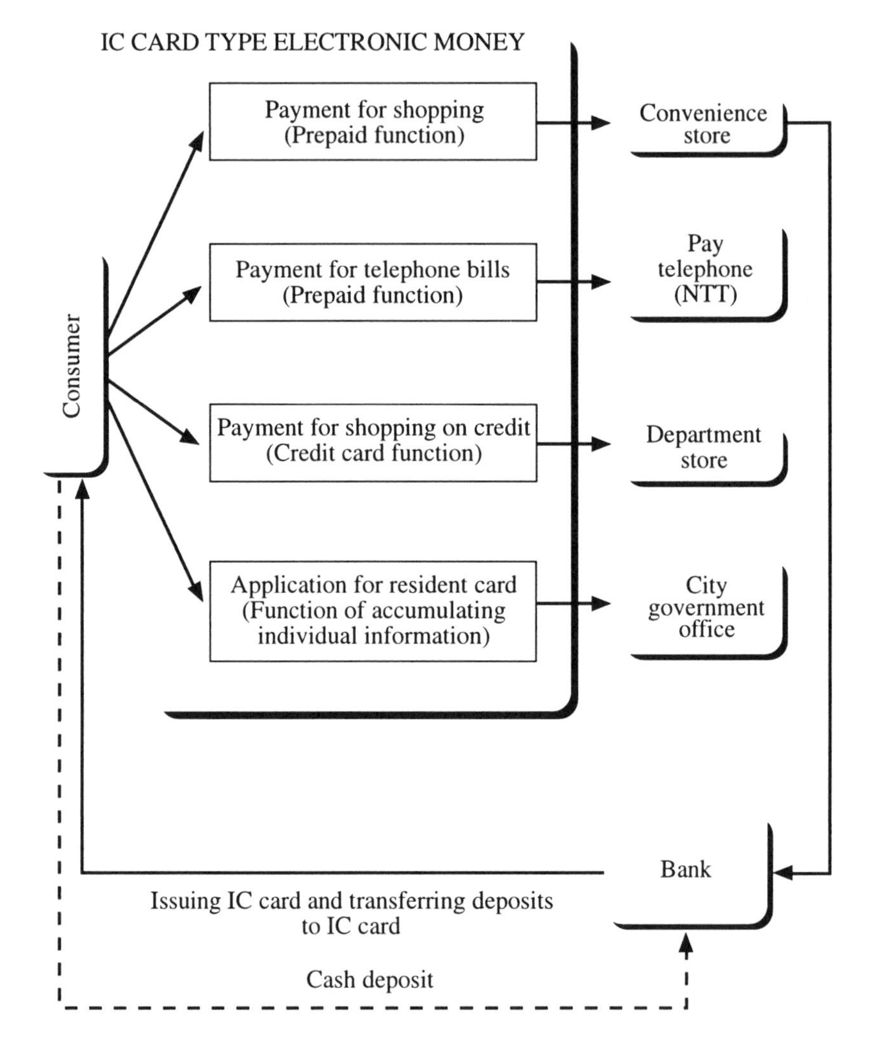

The IC card has an outward appearance of a bank card, but has an ultra compact microprocessor and memory imbedded in the card. The total amount of money possessed will be saved in the memory and customers can pay by inserting the IC card into the card reader at the store. The convenience store can connect this card reader to the POS terminal. The amount of money in the ATM can be repeatedly replenished by the IC card. Furthermore "IC card type electronic money" and "network type electronic money" will be integrated if replenishment of the amount of money is possible by using the computer connected with the network. The individual information and historical records of the use of the card can also be entered. If the information is in the memory, the card can be used as a credit card or even as an ID to issue a resident's card. The possibility of this multi-purpose use of a single IC card is highly exciting. Various kinds of prepaid cards, i.e., telephone cards or train cards issued by Japan Railway will have the possibility of being integrated into a single IC card. Since the commission levied when using a credit card will not be charged for electronic money, it will be suitable for payment of small sums. In addition, the preparation of small change at the store would no longer be required.

The "IC card type electronic money" has several problems such as complex security issues which are yet to be solved for future commercial practicality. However, "the age of electronic money" will no doubt arrive in the near future. It is said that when 7-Eleven started its information system development in 1977, built into the system was the prospect of the commercialization of electronic money. As an agent for payment acceptance of various bills, the convenience industry has already moved into the banking sector. When electronic money arrives, the convenience industry will be able to start new financial services being armed with multiple stores and information network. From the viewpoint of "integration of retail with banking sectors", we cannot neglect the future trends of electronic money.

Survival of Convenience Stores in the Age of Electronic Money

If electronic money has already arrived, the "integration of retailers with banking sectors" would have made more progress. Convenience chain stores with superior information networks and with their total number of stores should have far better advantages because they can provide customers with the "convenience near at hand" or the convenience of one-stop shopping.

For several years, the oligopoly of three major convenience chains has been expanding. With this affluent financial power background, the major convenience chains have established powerful information systems. So far, the information system has contributed to the efficiency in the operations of item-by-item management, and has offered new services. In future it will play an important role in transmitting financial information during the age of electronic money. With these changes, small convenience chains with inferior information systems will be dismissed from the market. At the same time, there will be no guarantee that these big three companies will survive, as superiority in hardware only is not enough for surviving the competition. Only enterprises which successfully take the side of "new changes" will be able to win the survival race.

Bibliography

1. Ishii Takatoshi, "Zusetsu Densi Money" (Illustration of electronic money), Toyo Keizai Shinposha, 1996.
2. Ishikawa Akira, "Senryaku Joho System Nyumon" (New Edition) (A guide to a strategic information system), Nihon Keizai Shimbun, 1997.
3. Iwafuchi Akio, "7-Eleven Akinaino Shin Jigen He" (7-Eleven Japan moves to a new dimension of business), OS Shuppan, 1993.
4. Uemura Takaki, "SIS no Jissai" (Practice of SIS), Nihon Keizai Shimbun, 1991.
5. Ogata Tomoyuki, "Suzuki Toshifumi ni manabu leader no jouken" (Conditions required for a leader learned from Suzuki Toshifumi), Yamato Shuppan, 1997.
6. Ogata Tomoyuki, "Ito-Yokado no gyokai part 3, merchandising kakumei he no chosen" (A challenge to merchandising revolution part 3, Ito-Yokado's business revolution), edited by 2020 AIM (published by Office 2020, 1992).
7. Kawabe Nobuo, "7-Eleven no Keieishi" (Management history of 7-Eleven Japan), Yuhikaku Publishing Co., 1994.
8. Kunitomo Ryuichi, "7-Eleven no joho kakumei" (The revolution of information system by 7-Eleven Japan), Pal Shuppan, 1997.
9. Takemura Kenichi, "Yumeni nozomu venture kigyouka" (Venture entrepreneur challenging for a dream), Taiyo Kikaku Shuppan, 1997.
10. Tajima Yoshiharu, Harada Hideki, "Seminar Ryutsu Nyumon" (A beginners' course on distribution).

11. "Ryutu keizai no tebiki" (A guide to a distribution economy — 1998), edited by Nihon Keizai Shimbun, 1997.
12. "Nikkei Financial — Kinyuha Kou Kawaru" (The Nikkei financial banking system will change this way), Nihon Keizai Shimbun, 1997.
13. Nomura Hidekazu, "Ito-Yokado 7-Eleven Japan", Otsuki Shoken, 1997.
14. Matsuyuki Yasuo, "Keizai Johoron" (A theory of economic information), Sosei Sha, 1993.
15. Yasaka Toshihiro, "Convenience store system no kakushinsei" (Innovativeness of convenience store system), Nihon Keizai Shimbun, 1994.
16. "Shinka suru POS system" (Progressing POS system), edited by Ryutsu System Kaihatsu Center, Nihon Keizai Shimbun, 1995.
17. "Shintei kyosou no senryaku" (Newly revised strategies for competition), M. E. Porter, Diamond Inc., 1995.
18. "Strategy and computer", C. Wiseman, Dow Jones–Irwin, 1995.
19. "Convenience store no subete" (Everything about convenience stores), Commercial Circles, 1995.
20. "Kombini" (Convenience) '95 Autumn issue, '96 Spring and Summer issues, '96 Winter issue, '97 Spring issue, '97 Summer issue, Commercial Circles.
21. "Shukan Diamond" (Weekly journal *Diamond*) '88, '97, Diamond Inc., 1988, 1997.
22. "Commercial Circles Special Edition '97", Commercial Circles, 1997.
23. "Nikkei Trendy", 1997 December issue, Nikkei Home Shuppan.
24. "Nikkei Information Strategy", December issue 1997, January issue 1998 by Nikkei BP.
25. "Nikkei Business", 9 December 1985 issue, PHP Institute, Inc., 1997.
26. "Nikkei Management Indicator", Nihon Keizai Shimbun, 92–97.
27. "List of Financial Statements — 7-Eleven Japan", Ministry of Finance, Printing Bureau, 1995–97.
28. "7-Eleven Japan Owarinaki Innovation" (7-Eleven Japan's endless innovation), 7-Eleven Japan, 1991.
29. Nihon Keizai Shimbun (newspaper).
30. Nikkei Ryutus Shimbun (newspaper).

Postscript

1997 was truly "the year of bankruptcies". While working on this book, we witnessed a series of high-profile failures of some of Japan's major institutions. These include Sanyo Securities Co., Hokkaido Takushoku Bank, Tokuyo City Bank, Ltd., and of course Yamaichi Securities Co., Ltd. Yaohan, once prosperous in the retail industry, also experienced a major financial crisis. Department stores and supermarkets could not break out of their long-term stagnant business performance. In comparison, the convenience industry seemed to be in very good health and high spirits.

None more so than 7-Eleven Japan, which achieved results of over 100 billion yen in ordinary profits for its 1997 accounts. It was the first time the domestic convenience industry had reached such an excellent level of profitability. It gives the impression that 7-Eleven Japan has excelled even its parent company Ito-Yokado, and has finally climbed up on the throne and is "king of the retail industry".

It is quite natural that the reasons behind 7-Eleven Japan's competitiveness and its methods used to achieve success have created such a strong interest worldwide. The main purpose of this book is to clarify some of the reasons behind this success. Many experts conclude that the main source of competitiveness for 7-Eleven Japan originates from its integrated information system. This view is not incorrect and we spent many pages in this book discussing its information system. The writers conclude that its key management concept of "response to change" has enabled 7-Eleven Japan to achieve such success. 7-Eleven Japan had been constantly developing its information system, building up the distribution system and creating new businesses, in order to cope with change.

Readers of this book will get ideas of how 7-Eleven Japan took change on its side and performed several self-reformations. We also believe company employees, who worry and fret about changes of external circumstances, i.e., deregulation and others, can learn many things from 7-Eleven Japan's ability to adapt itself to changes in its surroundings.

However, even blue-chip companies including 7-Eleven Japan experience many problems and have tasks yet to be solved. We pointed out such problems in this book and objectively analyzed them.

In the last two chapters, we tried to survey the future prospects of the entire convenience industry to which 7-Eleven Japan belongs. Convenience stores appeared in the 1970s and have been expanding their business by breaking the fetters of the existing retail business. 7-Eleven Japan has brought about a series of "revolutions" in the distribution system, information systems, the development of products, and the management of merchandise.

Toward the 21st century the change surrounding the retail business will be even more intense than before. We wonder whether the convenience industry could still be a "lucky adventurer" in the retail industry in future. We have tried to find some of the answers to this question from the viewpoint of the strategy of the convenience industry adapting to deregulation.

In the 1980s, Japan had been enjoying prosperity, but currently pessimism is the predominant sentiment. Not only within the retail industry but entire industries, companies, managers, and company employees are faced with "change" of the type they have never experienced before, hugely increasing their sense of uneasiness.

We intended to propose the essence of how to live through "the times of change" from the successful experiences of 7-Eleven Japan and the future prospects of the convenience store industry. If readers have received some hints on how to "take the challenge of change on your side", the purpose of this book is, to a great degree, fulfilled.

Index